BIBLE HISTORY

FOR YOUNG CATHOLICS

THE OLD TESTAMENT

WRITTEN BY
SETON STAFF

SETON PRESS
FRONT ROYAL, VA

Executive Editor: Dr. Mary Kay Clark
Editors: Seton Staff

Seton Home Study School
1350 Progress Drive
Front Royal, VA 22630
540-636-9990
540-636-1602 fax

For more information, visit us on the Web at http://www.setonhome.org.
Contact us by e-mail at info@setonhome.org.

ISBN: 978-1-60704-106-1

Cover: *Daniel in the Lions' Den,* Alfred Rethel

DEDICATED TO THE SACRED HEART OF JESUS

Contents

Chapter 1

The Creation of the World

God the Creator

The Eternal God Creates the World

Before there was anything, there was God. God always was. He always will be and He will always remain the same. That is why we say God is eternal.

God did not need to create anything. He is perfect. He is perfectly happy. He did not need to create anything to make Himself happy or to please Himself. However, God is all love. In His love, He decided to create beings to share in His happiness.

Thus, God created the heavens and the Earth. At first the Earth was empty and dark. Then God said, "Let there be light," and there was light. Then He separated the dark and the light. The light He called "day," and the dark He called "night." This was the first day of creation.

On the second day of creation, God created the skies.

On the third day, God created dry land. He separated the land from the water. He created the seas, the rivers, the lakes, and the oceans. He called the dry land the earth and the water the sea. Then with the eye of an artist, God created the plants, the trees, and the hundreds of thousands of beautiful flowers that are found all over the world. He filled the world with incredible color and beauty.

On the fourth day, God packed the skies with uncountable numbers of stars. He created the sun and the moon.

The next day, God created the millions of fish and other creatures that swim in the world's oceans, rivers, and lakes. He also created all the birds that fly through the air. All were different, unique, and fascinating.

On the sixth day of creation, God filled the land with all manner of animals. Then He said, "Let Us make man in Our Own Image and Likeness. And give him dominion over all the Earth." So God formed man out of the dust of the earth and breathed an immortal soul into him. God called this first man "Adam."

God looked at all the wonders that He had created and saw that they were good. So on the seventh day, He rested.

The Creation of the Garden of Paradise

After God had created the heavens and the Earth, He planted a magnificent garden. This was an Earthly paradise with all kinds of wonderful plants and animals. In the middle of the garden, He planted two special trees. One was the Tree of Life. The other was the Tree of Knowledge of Good and Evil. God told Adam that he could eat the fruit of every tree in the garden but one. Adam could not eat the fruit of the Tree of Knowledge of Good and Evil. God warned Adam that if he ate the fruit of this tree that he would die.

Then God brought all the animals that He had created to Adam so that Adam could name them. God had created male and female animals, but he had not created a companion for Adam. God saw that though Adam was happy in the garden, he was lonely. God saw that it was not good for Adam to be alone. Thus God decided to create a companion for Adam.

God put Adam into a deep sleep. While Adam was sleeping, God took a rib from Adam's side. God chose the side, not the head or the foot, to show that the companion was to be Adam's equal, neither above him nor below him. From the rib, God formed a woman. When Adam woke up, God brought the woman to Adam. Adam named her "Eve," which means the mother of all the living.

Adam and Eve were very happy in the Garden of Paradise. They loved each other and they loved God. The fruit from the Tree of Life kept them from becoming sick or from dying.

The Fall of the Angels

In addition to the physical world, God also created a spiritual world. The creations of this world are the angels. At first, the angels were happy. They worshiped God and sang His praises.

God did not make all the angels equal. The brightest and greatest of the angels was named "Lucifer." His name means "Light bearer." At some point, Lucifer became so proud of himself that he began to imagine that he was as great as God. Sadly, he revolted against God. Other angels also committed the sin of pride and joined Lucifer in his revolt. The archangel Michael led the angels who remained faithful to God. They fought against Lucifer and the bad angels and cast them out of Heaven. With God's help, Michael cast Lucifer and the evil angels into Hell. Lucifer was now called Satan and the evil angels were called devils.

As Satan suffered in Hell, he cast his eyes on Adam and Eve in their garden. Satan raged with anger and misery. He was determined that Adam and Eve would join him in his suffering. He planned to make them disobey God.

Chapter Review

Fill in the blanks to complete the sentences below.

1. God always was, always will be, and will always remain the same which is why we say God is _eternal_ .

2. In the middle of the Garden of Paradise, God planted two special trees: _The Tree of Life_ and _The tree of Knowledge_ . of good and evil.

3. God chose to make Eve from Adam's _rib_ to show that she was to be his equal.

4. The brightest and greatest of the angels was _Lucifer_ , whose name means "Light bearer."

5. With God's help, the archangel _Michael_ cast into Hell Satan and all the other evil angels.

Chapter 2

Man's Sin and God's Punishment

Adam and Eve Are Cast Out of the Garden

The Fall of Adam and Eve

One day as Eve walked in the garden, she came upon the Tree of Knowledge of Good and Evil. As she looked at the tree, a serpent approached her. The serpent asked her why she did not eat the fruit of the tree. The serpent was Satan in disguise.

Eve told the serpent that God had told her not to eat the fruit of the tree. She said that if she ate the fruit that she would die. Satan is clever. He is the father of lies. So he said to Eve that God had not told her the truth. She and Adam would not die if they ate the fruit. In fact, they would be like gods. Their eyes would be opened and she and Adam would know the secret of good and evil.

As Eve looked at the juicy fruit on the tree, she became curious. The more she looked, the better and more delicious the forbidden fruit looked. Finally, she plucked the fruit off the tree and took a bite. Then she gave it to her husband Adam who also ate some of the fruit. This was their first sin. It was the original sin, a sin of disobedience.

All at once, their eyes *were* opened. Yet, it was not as Satan had promised. They felt shame for what they had done. They gathered fig leaves and sewed them together to make clothes. Then they hid from God.

Adam and Eve Are Cast Out of the Garden, but God Promises a Redeemer

In the evening, God came into the garden as He did every evening. He called to Adam and Eve as a loving father calls to his children. Like a child who knows he has done something wrong, Adam feared answering God. Yet God called them to come to Him. When Adam approached, God asked him what was wrong. Adam said that he had eaten the fruit of the forbidden tree. However, he blamed Eve for giving him the fruit. When God asked Eve why she had eaten the forbidden fruit, she blamed the serpent.

Then God turned to the serpent (Satan). He told the snake that for the rest of time, he would crawl on his belly and eat the dust. God also promised that He would send a Redeemer to save Adam and Eve and all their descendants. He told Satan that there would be enmity between him and the Redeemer.

God told Adam and Eve that for their sin of disobedience, they would die. He also told them that their lives would be hard. Then God made clothes for them out of animal skins and drove them out of the Garden of Paradise. He placed an angel with a flaming sword at the entrance to the Garden so that they could never return.

Cain and Abel

Adam and Eve had many children. Their oldest two were boys named Cain and Abel. Cain and Abel were very different. Cain was a farmer and, sadly, a bad person. Abel was a shepherd who was kind and generous.

To thank God for blessing their harvest, Cain and Abel each offered God a sacrifice. Abel sacrificed one of his finest lambs. Cain offered fruit from his farms. However, unlike Abel, Cain did not sacrifice his best fruit. Thus, Abel's sacrifice pleased God, but Cain's did not.

When Cain saw that his sacrifice displeased God, he became angry with Abel. In a loving tone, God told Cain that he needed to work on overcoming his sins. If he did, then God would be as pleased with him as He was with Abel. Yet, Cain remained jealous of his brother. One day, Cain asked Abel to go with him into the fields. Cain attacked Abel and killed him.

God knew that Cain had committed a terrible sin. He asked Cain where Abel was. Cain said that he did not know. He said that he was not his brother's keeper. God told Cain that He knew he had killed Abel. God told Cain that for murdering his brother, Cain would have to wander the Earth as a fugitive for the rest of his life.

To comfort Adam and Eve for the loss of Abel, God blessed them with another son: Seth. Seth was a good and holy man. His children and descendants followed the laws of God. Cain's children and his descendents were wicked and evil. Thus, the world was divided into good people and bad people.

Noah and the Flood

Over the decades, the world became more and more wicked. Before long, only Noah and his family obeyed God and His laws. So God told Noah to build a large boat called an Ark. God told Noah that in a hundred years when the Ark was finished, He would send a flood to destroy the world.

For one hundred years, Noah built the Ark. At the same time, he preached to the people. He urged them to repent. Sadly, the people just laughed at Noah.

When Noah finished the Ark, God told Noah to take his family into the Ark. He also told Noah to gather two of every animal and take them into the Ark. Then God sent a terrible flood upon the Earth. The water covered the highest mountains. Yet the Ark floated peacefully on the water. All life on Earth perished. Only Noah, his family, and the animals in the Ark stayed alive.

The Sacrifice of Noah

After the flood had covered the world for 150 days, God sent a warm wind to evaporate the waters. After seven months, the Ark came to rest on Mount Ararat (in modern Turkey). To see if water still covered the Earth, Noah sent out a raven, which did not return. Then he sent out a dove, which did return to the Ark. A week later, he sent the dove again. This time, the dove returned with a branch from an olive tree. Noah knew that the floodwaters had evaporated from the Earth. God commanded that Noah and his family and all the animals leave the Ark, which had been their home and refuge for a year.

To thank God, Noah built an altar. On the altar, he offered a sacrifice to God. Noah's sacrifice pleased God, Who blessed him and his sons. God made a promise to Noah, his sons, and all their descendents. The Lord promised that never again would the Earth be destroyed by water. As a sign of His promise, God set a rainbow in the sky.

The Tower of Babel

Over time, Noah's sons had children and those children had children. Before long, the descendents of Noah were so numerous that they could no longer live in the same area. Yet, rather than moving apart, their pride caused them to decide to build a tower to Heaven. Yet God easily stopped this foolish project. Suddenly, their language was confused. They could not understand one another. Before this, they had all spoken the same language.

Now they spoke many different languages. They abandoned the tower. The people spread over the Earth.

Chapter Review

Fill in the blanks to complete the sentences below.

1. Satan appeared as a _serpent_ to tempt Eve.

2. After Adam and Eve sinned, God promised to send _a Redeemer_.

3. _Cain_ was the first murderer.

4. After seven months, Noah's Ark came to rest on _Mount Ararat_.

5. The _rainbow_ is a sign of God's promise never to destroy the Earth again by water.

Chapter 3

The Father of Nations: Abraham

Abraham Gathers Up His Family

God Calls Forth Abraham

At Haran, in the middle of the world that had become very evil, lived a good and holy man named Abraham. God chose Abraham to keep alive the message that He would send a Redeemer. Thus, God told Abraham to leave Haran and his relatives and go to a distant land. God promised Abraham that He would make him the father of a great nation.

Abraham obeyed God. He gathered up his wife Sarah and his nephew Lot along with his servants and his herds. Then Abraham moved to the land of Canaan – a land flowing with milk and honey. God spoke to Abraham and promised to give him and his descendants the land of Canaan. In thanksgiving, Abraham built an altar and made a sacrifice to God.

Lot and Abraham Part Ways

As the herds of Lot and Abraham grew larger, there was less and less grazing land for their cattle. Disputes arose among Lot's servants and Abraham's. To avoid more quarrels, Abraham and Lot decided to part. Lot chose the land around the Jordan River and lived in the city of Sodom. Abraham returned to Hebron.

Abraham Rescues Lot

Soon after Lot and Abraham parted ways, foreign kings invaded the area where Lot lived. These kings sacked the cities of Sodom and Gomorrah. They took Lot hostage and stole all his possessions.

When Abraham heard that Lot had been kidnapped, he gathered three hundred eighteen of his servants. He set off in pursuit of the bandit kings. When Abraham found them, he defeated them and rescued Lot and recovered his goods. Then he returned Lot to his lands.

Abraham Meets Melchizedek

As Abraham was returning home, he met Melchizedek. Melchizedek was a king of Salem and priest of the Lord. He offered a sacrifice of bread and wine and blessed Abraham.

God Makes a Promise to Abraham

One night God called Abraham to the door of his tent. He told Abraham to look at the stars in the sky. God promised Abraham that one day his descendants would be as numerous as the stars.

Melchizedek Offers Bread and Wine

Another time God spoke to Abraham. On this occasion, God made a covenant (a special pledge) with Abraham. God renewed His promise that Abraham would be the father of many nations. In return for His promise, God asked that Abraham always obey Him faithfully. Then God made Abraham a wonderful promise. God promised that He would give Abraham and Sarah a son whom they should name Isaac.

Abraham Has Special visitors

One hot day, three strangers were walking towards Abraham's tent. When Abraham saw them, he bowed down and spoke to the leader. Abraham told the man that if he would rest under the shade of a nearby tree, he would bring the three men some bread and drink so that they could refresh themselves.

While the men rested in the shade, Sarah began to bake the bread. From his flocks, Abraham chose a young calf, which he ordered his servants to cook. When the bread and the calf were cooked, Abraham took milk and butter and served the delicious food to the three men.

Abraham Has Special Visitors

After they had eaten, the leader of the three men told Abraham that they would return again in a year. He said that when they returned, Sarah would have a baby boy. When the man said this, Abraham knew that this was God Himself, and that the other two men were His angels.

The Destruction of Sodom and Gomorrah

As God and the angels departed, the Lord told Abraham that He was going to destroy Sodom and Gomorrah because the people in these cities were very wicked. Abraham was filled with love for the people in these cities. He begged God not to kill the innocent along with the guilty. He asked God that if there were fifty innocents in the city not to destroy the city. God agreed. When the Lord agreed not to destroy the cities for the sake of fifty innocents, Abraham asked God again, would He save the cities if there were forty innocents? Finally, the Lord agreed that, if even ten innocent people were found in Sodom and Gomorrah, He would not destroy the cities.

Unfortunately, not even ten innocent people could be found in the two cities. Thus, the next day, the Lord prepared to destroy Sodom and Gomorrah. First, He sent two angels to escort Lot, his wife, and his two daughters from Sodom. Then the Lord sent a rain of fire down upon the cities, utterly consuming them.

Lot and his family had been warned by the angels not to look back at the city. However, Lot's wife disobeyed the angels' command. When she looked back, she instantly turned into a pillar of salt. The area around Sodom and Gomorrah became a sulphurous lake known as the "Dead Sea." It stands as a sign to those who disobey God.

Chapter Review

Fill in the blanks to complete the sentences below.

1. Lot was Abraham's _nephew_.

2. Melchizedek offered a sacrifice of _bread_ and _wine_ when he met Abraham.

3. A covenant is a _special pledge_

4. When Lot's wife disobeyed the angels' command, she instantly turned into _a pillar of salt_.

5. The area around Sodom and Gomorrah is a sulphurous lake known as _the Dead Sea_.

A Father Offers Up His Son: Isaac

Abraham Offers Up His Son Isaac

Abraham and Isaac

After God destroyed Sodom and Gomorrah, Sarah gave birth to a baby boy. Abraham named his son Isaac. Abraham loved Isaac very deeply because Isaac had been born when he and Sarah were very old. Abraham knew that Isaac was the last child he and Sarah would ever have together.

One day, God decided to test Abraham. God wanted Abraham to prove that he loved God more than he loved his son. So God commanded Abraham to take Isaac to a mountain in the land of Moria and sacrifice him.

Abraham did not hesitate. He cut wood and placed it on a donkey. Then he took Isaac and two servants and began the journey to the mountain.

As he approached the mountain, Abraham ordered the servants to stay behind. Then he put the wood on Isaac's shoulders and the two of them began to climb the mountain. As they climbed, Isaac became curious. He told his father that he saw that they had the wood and the fire, but they had nothing to sacrifice. Abraham told him that God would provide a sacrifice.

When Abraham arrived at the place God told him about, Abraham built an altar. He put the wood on the altar. Then Abraham tied the hands of his only son whom he loved so much. He placed Isaac

on the altar. Then Abraham raised his great knife to sacrifice his son to God.

Just as Abraham was about to strike, an angel grabbed his wrist. The angel told him not to hurt Isaac. The angel said that God was satisfied. For love of God, Abraham was willing to sacrifice his only son. As Abraham freed Isaac, Abraham noticed a ram caught in a bramble bush. Capturing the ram, Abraham sacrificed it to God.

Isaac Marries Rebecca

When Isaac became old enough to marry, Abraham wanted to make certain that he married a woman who believed in God and would be a good wife. So Abraham called his most trusted servant, a man named Eliezer. Abraham told Eliezer to return to Haran to find a wife for Isaac among Abraham's people. Eliezer loaded ten camels with goods and left for Haran.

As Eliezer approached Haran, he had the camels lie down outside the city walls. Each day, the women of the city would come out to draw water from the well that was outside the walls. Eliezer prayed to God to help him find a wife for Isaac. He prayed that the woman that Isaac should marry would offer him a drink of water and also offer to give water to his camels.

Eliezer had barely finished his prayer when a beautiful young woman carrying a pitcher walked up to the well. Her name was Rebecca. After she had filled her pitcher with water, Eliezer asked her for a drink. She gave him a drink and offered to water his camels while he drank. When Eliezer heard this he was amazed. He stood silently as she gave water to his camels.

When Rebecca finished watering the camels, Eliezer asked who she was. She told him. She also told him that he was welcome to stay in her father's home. Eliezer realized that God had answered his prayer. Rebecca was the wife for Isaac.

Eliezar went with Rebecca to her father's house. He told her father and her brother Laban that he had come to Haran to find a wife for Isaac. He told them about his prayer. Rebecca's father agreed that it was God's will that Rebecca marry Isaac. After an exchange of gifts and a great banquet, Rebecca returned with Eliezer to marry Isaac.

The marriage of Isaac and Rebecca filled Abraham with great joy. Abraham lived to be 175 years old. God blessed him all the days of his life.

Eliezer Meets Rebecca

Chapter Review

Fill in the blanks to complete the sentences below.

1. ___Isaac___ was Abraham's son.

2. Abraham sent his trusted servant ___Eliezer___ to Haran to find a wife for his son.

3. Abraham's son married ___Rebecca___ .

Chapter 5

The Man Who Wrestled An Angel: Jacob

Esau Sells His Birthright for a Bowl of Soup

The Sons of Isaac: Jacob and Esau

God blessed Isaac and Rebecca with twin sons. Though they were twins, the two boys were quite different. Isaac and Rebecca named their first son Esau. Esau grew to become a big man, with lots of red hair. He had hairy arms and legs. He was rough in his manners and his speech. Esau was a hunter.

Isaac and Rebecca named their second son Jacob. Jacob was very different from his twin brother. He had smooth skin and a gentle nature. Jacob became a shepherd when he grew up.

Isaac loved both his sons very much. Yet he seemed to care more for Esau. Isaac loved Esau's boldness and daring. He enjoyed eating the game that Esau killed when he went hunting. Rebecca also loved her two sons, but she cared more for Jacob. God had told her that one day Jacob would rule over Esau.

One day, Esau, who had been out hunting, returned home very hungry. Jacob had just finished cooking a lentil (bean) soup. When the hungry Esau smelled the delicious soup, he asked Jacob for it. However, Jacob refused to give him the soup unless Esau sold him his birthright -- his inheritance and place of honor in the family. Esau did not think anything of the matter and sold his birthright to Jacob.

Years later, when Isaac had grown very old and gone blind, he called Esau to his bedside. He asked Esau to go hunting for him one final time and cook him a delicious meal from the animal he would kill. Isaac told Esau that after the meal, he would give him a final blessing before he died. Rebecca, who had overheard this conversation, called Jacob as soon as Esau had left. She told Jacob to kill two young lambs so that she could cook a meal for Isaac. Then he could take the meal to his father and receive Isaac's blessing instead of his brother.

At first, Jacob told his mother that he would not deceive his father. He feared that Isaac would discover that Jacob had deceived him and that, instead of a blessing, he would receive a curse from Isaac. However, Rebecca convinced him. She clothed him in the skin of one of the young lambs and sent him in to see Isaac.

When Jacob, pretending to be Esau, spoke to his father, Isaac doubted it was Esau. So he called his son to his bedside. He touched his hands and arms. Isaac said that it was Jacob's voice, but Esau's hands and arms. So, believing it was Esau, Isaac ate the meal and blessed Jacob.

Jacob Pretends to be Esau

Jacob had barely left his father's tent when Esau returned from the hunt. When he heard what Jacob had done, he was furious! He accused Jacob of robbing him first of his birthright and now his father's final blessing. From that moment, Esau hated Jacob and threatened to kill him. Rebecca, fearing for Jacob's life, told him to flee to Haran where he could live with her brother Laban until Esau's anger cooled. Jacob agreed and left for Haran.

Jacob's Dream

As Jacob traveled to Haran, night fell. Worn out and tired, Jacob lay down. He took a stone and put it under his head as a pillow. While he slept, he had a dream. In the dream, he saw a ladder which rested on the earth but which reached up to Heaven. Angels went up and down the ladder. At the top of the ladder was God the Father. God spoke to Jacob. He told Jacob that He would give him and his descendants the land upon which Jacob slept.

When Jacob awoke, he took his stone pillow and set it up as a marker. He poured oil on it and dedicated the place to God. He called the place "Bethel," which means "the house of God."

Jacob Meets Rachel and Laban

Continuing his journey, Jacob arrived at a well where three flocks of sheep rested. He approached the shepherds and asked them if they knew Laban. They said that they did. They pointed to a pretty young woman who they said was Laban's daughter Rachel. Rachel was driving a flock of sheep to the well. When Jacob saw

her, he ran to the well to remove the stone that covered the well. He helped her water her sheep and told her who he was.

When Rachel heard that Jacob was her cousin, she ran home to tell her father Laban. Laban came out to the well to meet Jacob. Laban took Jacob back to his home.

Jacob Meets Rachel

Jacob lived with Laban for twenty years caring for Laban's flocks. Under Jacob's supervision, Laban's herds greatly increased. Laban often tried to cheat Jacob, but God blessed Jacob until he became a very wealthy man. During this time, Jacob tried to marry Rachel. However, Laban put many obstacles in Jacob's path so that it was many years before Jacob was able to marry Rachel whom he loved very much.

Jacob and Esau Meet

After twenty years with Laban, God commanded Jacob to take his family, his servants, and his cattle and move back home. Jacob obeyed God. As Jacob neared Canaan, he began to fear that Esau might still wish to kill him. He sent messengers to his brother to make peace with him. Instead of sending back an answer with the messengers, Esau came himself at the head of a band of four hundred men.

When Jacob heard that Esau was coming with four hundred men, he was very afraid. He prayed to God to save him from Esau. During the night, an angel appeared to Jacob and wrestled with him until the morning. At daybreak, the angel told Jacob to let him go. However, Jacob refused to release him until the angel blessed him. The angel said that because Jacob had wrestled successfully with an angel, he would be renamed "Israel." Before he left, the angel blessed him.

As the dawn broke across the land, Jacob (Israel) saw Esau and his men in the distance. Jacob divided his family and his servants and his herds into two groups. Then he went to meet Esau. As he approached Esau, Jacob bowed before him. The two brothers hugged and wept for joy at the reunion. Jacob's children also came forward and bowed before Esau.

After a short time, the two brothers parted. Jacob continued his journey to Canaan. When Isaac met Jacob, he was filled with joy. Isaac thanked God that his son had returned. Isaac lived to be 180 years old. When he died, Jacob and Esau buried him.

Chapter Review

Fill in the blanks to complete the sentences below.

1. Isaac and Rebecca's two sons were _Jacob_ and _Esau_.

2. _Esau_ sold _Jacob_ his birthright for a bowl of soup.

3. Rebecca convinced _Jacob_ to deceive his father Isaac.

4. _Jacob_ married Rachel.

5. After wrestling all night with an angel, the angel said that _Jacob_ would be renamed _Israel_.

The Dreamer: Joseph

Joseph's Brothers Throw Him into an Empty Pit

Joseph's Brothers Hate Him

Jacob had twelve sons but he loved his son Joseph most of all. One day, Jacob had a coat of many colors made for Joseph. When his brothers saw the magnificent coat, they became very angry and envious of Joseph. One day, as the brothers tended their herds, they did something very bad. Joseph told Jacob what his brothers had done. This also made the brothers hate Joseph.

Another time, Joseph told his brothers about a dream that he had. In the dream, they were all binding sheaves of wheat in the field. Suddenly, his sheaf rose up and their sheaves all bowed down to his sheaf. His brothers asked him if he meant to rule over them. They hated him even more because of the dream and what he had said.

Yet again Joseph had a dream that he related to his brothers. In this dream, the sun, the moon, and eleven stars bowed down to him. This time, even Jacob became angry. Jacob asked if the dream meant that he, his mother, and his brothers would bow down to him. His brothers became angrier, but Jacob began to think about the dream. He began to wonder if God had great things planned for Joseph.

Joseph Is Sold Into Slavery

Some days later, Joseph's brothers went to graze their flocks at Shechem. Jacob told Joseph to go and see how his brothers were doing. When they saw Joseph coming, they plotted to kill him. They planned to attack Joseph, kill him, and throw his body into a pit. Then they would return to Jacob and say that a wild animal had eaten him. However, Reuben, the oldest brother, did not want to kill Joseph. He suggested that they put Joseph into the pit alive. Reuben hoped that he could return later to rescue Joseph.

As soon as Joseph reached his brothers, they grabbed him and took his many-colored coat. Then they threw him into the empty pit. As they sat down to eat, a caravan of Ishmaelite merchants on their way to Egypt happened to pass by. Judah suggested to his brothers that there was nothing to gain by killing Joseph and reminded them that, after all, he *was* their brother. It would be a better idea to sell him. So they pulled him out of the well and sold him for twenty pieces of silver to the Ishmaelites who took Joseph to Egypt.

Reuben had not been present when Joseph was sold. When he returned to his brothers' camp, he looked for Joseph. Not finding him, Reuben asked what had happened to him. The other brothers ignored him.

Then the brothers killed a goat and dipped Joseph's coat in the blood. They took the coat back to Jacob and told him that they had found it. Jacob knew it was Joseph's coat. He thought that some ferocious animal had killed Joseph. Jacob tore his clothes and began to weep.

Joseph in Potiphar's House

When the Ishmaelites reached Egypt, they sold Joseph to Potiphar. Potiphar was the captain of Pharaoh's guards. Since God was with Joseph, he succeeded in all that he did. Potiphar saw that Joseph was a good and trustworthy servant. He put Joseph in charge of his entire household. Soon, Potiphar became wealthy because of Joseph.

One day, Potiphar's wife tried to make Joseph commit a sin. Yet he would not sin. Day after day, this bad woman tried to make Joseph sin, but he would not. One day, as he ran away from her, she grabbed his cloak. When Potiphar came home that night, she lied about Joseph. She said that he had tried to attack her. She showed Potiphar Joseph's cloak as proof of the attack. Sadly, Potiphar believed her story. He became very angry with Joseph and had him thrown into prison.

Joseph in Prison

In prison, God continued to watch over and bless Joseph. Soon he was placed in charge of other prisoners. One day, Pharaoh had two of his servants, his cupbearer and his baker, thrown into prison for offending him. The prison warden assigned them to Joseph.

One night, the baker and the cupbearer each had a dream that upset them. In the morning, Joseph saw that they were upset. He asked them why they were sad. They said that they had had dreams but there was no one who could tell them what the dreams meant. Joseph asked them to tell him their dreams.

The cupbearer said that in his dream, there were three branches of a vine that slowly grew and blossomed into grapes. Then he took the grapes and made them into wine that he gave to Pharaoh to drink. When Joseph heard the dream, he told the cupbearer what the dream meant. Joseph said that in three days, Pharaoh would restore the cupbearer to his former position. Joseph also begged the cupbearer to remember him when he saw Pharaoh. Joseph asked him to speak to Pharaoh on his behalf and tell Pharaoh that, though he was in prison, he was innocent of any crime.

Then the baker told Joseph his dream. In the baker's dream, he was carrying three baskets of bread. In the top basket were all kinds of baked goods for Pharaoh, but birds were eating the food. With great sorrow, Joseph told him that his dream meant that in three days, Pharaoh would order that he be killed.

Three days later, everything happened exactly as Joseph had said it would. Pharaoh ordered the baker to be executed and the cupbearer restored to his former position. The cupbearer, however, forgot about Joseph who remained in prison.

Pharaoh's Dreams

About two years later, Pharaoh had a dream. In the dream, he was standing on the banks of the Nile River. Up from the river came seven fat cows. They began to graze along the banks of the river. Then seven thin, ugly cows came up from the river. The thin cows ate the fat cows. Then Pharaoh awoke.

Pharaoh fell asleep and again had a dream. In this dream, he saw seven ears of corn. The ears of corn were large and healthy. Then seven other ears of corn grew, but this corn was thin and wasted. The thin corn ate up the healthy corn. Again, Pharaoh awoke.

In the morning, Pharaoh was troubled. He called together his wise men and told them his dreams but none could tell him what they meant. Then the cupbearer remembered

Joseph Interprets Dreams in Prison

Joseph. He told Pharaoh how Joseph had interpreted his dream and the baker's. Pharaoh sent for Joseph at once.

When Pharaoh told Joseph his dreams, Joseph told Pharaoh that he could not tell him what they meant, but that God could. The seven fat cows and seven healthy ears of corn represented seven years of plentiful harvests in Egypt. The seven thin cows and wasted corn represented seven years of famine. Joseph advised Pharaoh to choose a wise man and

make him ruler over all of Egypt. During the years of plenty, Joseph said the crops should be gathered into granaries in preparation for the years of famine so that the people would not starve to death.

Joseph Interprets Pharaoh's Dreams

Chapter Review

Fill in the blanks to complete the sentences below.

1. Jacob had <u>twelve</u> sons.

2. What gift did Jacob give to his son Joseph? <u>A coat of many colors.</u>

3. In Egypt, Joseph was sold to <u>Potiphar</u>, the captain of Pharaoh's guards.

4. In prison, Joseph interpreted dreams for Pharaoh's <u>baker</u> and <u>cupbearer</u>.

5. Pharaoh had two dreams, one about <u>cows</u> and one about <u>corn</u>.

The Ruler of Egypt: Joseph

Joseph is Placed in Charge of Egypt

Joseph in Charge of Egypt

Joseph's plan and advice deeply impressed Pharaoh. He greatly admired Joseph's wisdom and understanding of the problem. He told Joseph that he was the man who should be the ruler of Egypt. Joseph would be his second-in-command. Only the Pharaoh himself would be above Joseph. Then Pharaoh took the signet ring from his finger and placed it on Joseph's finger. He dressed Joseph in the finest clothes and placed a heavy gold chain around Joseph's neck. A herald went before Joseph shouting to the people that Joseph was in charge of all Egypt. Joseph was thirty years old when he entered Pharaoh's service.

Joseph Meets His Brothers

During the seven years of bounty, Joseph stored up huge amounts of grain. Then the famine struck! The people demanded grain from Pharaoh, but he told them to see Joseph and follow his orders. Joseph opened the granaries and gave people grain. In Egypt, no one starved; however, in other lands, the famine was dreadful.

In Canaan, the famine caused terrible suffering. Jacob, when he heard that there was grain in Egypt, sent ten of his sons to buy grain. Jacob did not send Benjamin, his youngest, because he was afraid that some harm might come to him.

When the brothers arrived in Egypt, they were taken before Joseph who was in charge of selling the grain. They bowed down before him. Joseph knew who they were but they did not recognize him. He pretended that he was a stranger and asked them harshly from where they came.

Then Joseph said that they were spies. The frightened brothers denied that they

were spies. They said that they had come only to buy wheat. They said that they had originally been twelve brothers but one brother was now dead and the youngest brother was back at home with their father. Joseph told them that he did not believe them and threw them into prison.

For three days, Joseph kept his brothers in prison. When he released them, he told them that one of them had to remain, but that the others should return to Canaan and bring their youngest brother back with them. This would prove whether they told the truth. The ten began to speak to each other not realizing that Joseph, who had only spoken through an interpreter, could understand them. They spoke of Joseph and how they had mistreated him so many years ago. They acknowledged that their treatment now was God's just punishment for their cruelty to Joseph. When Joseph heard how they had changed, he left the room and began to cry.

When Joseph returned, he had Simeon tied up and put into prison. Joseph had his servants load sacks of grain onto his brothers' donkeys but secretly returned all the money that they had paid for the grain. He also gave them provisions for their journey back home. When they were ready, his brothers left.

When the brothers arrived back home in Canaan, they went to Jacob and told him what had happened in Egypt. Then they emptied out their sacks of grain and found the money inside. When they saw the money, all of them became very alarmed. Jacob began to weep. He told the brothers that they were depriving him

Joseph Meets His Brothers

of his children. He cried that Joseph was dead, Simeon had been arrested, and now they wanted to take away Benjamin.

Joseph's Brothers Return to Egypt

When the brothers and their families had eaten all the grain that they had brought back from Egypt, Jacob told his sons to return to Egypt for more grain. However, Judah told his father that it was a waste of time and would be dangerous to return unless they took Benjamin with them. After a long discussion, Jacob finally, unwillingly, agreed to let Benjamin go. So the brothers took Benjamin, and twice as much money, and started back to Egypt.

When the brothers arrived in Egypt and Joseph saw Benjamin, he ordered his steward to take the brothers to his home to have a meal with him. The servant did as he was commanded. The brothers, though, were very worried. They feared that they were going to be attacked and sold as slaves because of the money that they had found in their sacks. They told the steward that they had brought the money back as well as additional money to buy more food. The steward told them not to worry. In fact, he brought Simeon to them.

When Joseph came home, the brothers bowed down before him and gave him the money and gifts that they had brought with them. He asked how they were. He also asked about their father, whether he was alive and if he were in good health. When they told him that Jacob lived, Joseph was very happy.

Then Joseph saw his beloved brother Benjamin. Joseph was so happy that he left the room and went outside to cry for joy. When he returned, he ordered his servants to serve the meal.

When Joseph seated them at the table, he placed them from oldest to youngest. This caused his brothers to be quite amazed. Each brother was served a large portion of food, but to Benjamin, Joseph gave five times as large a portion. Joseph and his brothers feasted and drank and had a wonderful meal together.

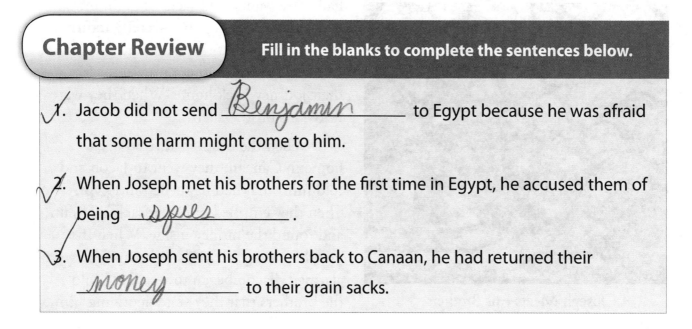

Chapter Review

Fill in the blanks to complete the sentences below.

1. Jacob did not send __Benjamin__ to Egypt because he was afraid that some harm might come to him.

2. When Joseph met his brothers for the first time in Egypt, he accused them of being __spies__ .

3. When Joseph sent his brothers back to Canaan, he had returned their __money__ to their grain sacks.

Chapter 8

The Family Reunited: Joseph

From Benjamin's Sack Came the Shining Silver Cup

The Silver Cup

Joseph wanted to test his brothers to see if they were as jealous of Benjamin as they had been of him. After the meal, Joseph called his steward. He told the steward to fill each brother's sack with grain and also to return each man's money to his sack. In Benjamin's sack, Joseph ordered that the steward place Joseph's own special silver cup. The steward hastened to obey.

The next morning, the brothers began their journey back to Canaan. They had barely left when Joseph ordered his steward to go after them and charge them with stealing his silver cup. He had his brothers dragged before him and accused them of the crime. He told them that whoever had the cup would be killed. The brothers were filled with terror for their lives. Quickly they opened their sacks and dumped out the contents. From Benjamin's sack came the shining silver cup.

The sight of the gleaming cup shocked the brothers. They threw themselves at Joseph's feet. Judah declared that they had no excuse. He said that they were being justly punished for their sins. Judah said that from now on, they would all be Joseph's slaves. However, Joseph said that only the one in whose sack the cup had been found should be his slave. The others could go.

When Judah heard Joseph's words, he pleaded with Joseph. He explained how difficult it had been for Jacob to let Benjamin come to Egypt. Judah told Joseph that he had promised to keep Benjamin safe even if it cost Judah his own life. He told Joseph that if they returned without Benjamin, it would kill Jacob. Then Judah offered himself as a slave in place of Benjamin.

Joseph Reveals Himself

Joseph now knew for certain that his brothers had changed. He ordered all his servants to leave the room. Then, bursting into tears, he said to his brothers, "I am Joseph." His brothers, filled with terror, could not answer him. Yet he spoke kindly to them and assured them that everything that they had done to him had been the Will of God. Then he asked how Jacob was. He told them to return to their father to tell him of his glory in Egypt. He also told them to gather their families and to return to Egypt because five years of famine still remained.

When Pharaoh heard the news of Joseph's brothers, he also told them to bring their families to Egypt where they would receive the best land to raise their herds and crops. Then Joseph sent his brothers to fetch Jacob. He sent them away with carts loaded with provisions as well as money and costly clothes.

Jacob Comes to Egypt

When Joseph's brothers told Jacob that Joseph lived and ruled Egypt, he did not believe them. However, when he saw the carts filled with silver and food, he was convinced. He determined to journey to Egypt to see Joseph before he died.

Jacob gathered up all his possessions and his sons and their wives and children and started the journey to Egypt. In all, seventy people traveled to Egypt. When the caravan arrived at the border of Canaan, God appeared to Jacob and told him not to be afraid. God promised Jacob that He would be with Jacob in Egypt. God also promised that Jacob's descendents would become a great nation and that one day, God would return them to Canaan.

Judah went ahead of the others to tell Joseph that Jacob was coming. Joseph had his chariot prepared and went out to meet his father in Goshen. As soon as Joseph saw his father, he threw his arms around him and began to weep for joy. Jacob told his son that he was now ready to die because he had seen that his son still lived.

Joseph then took Jacob and five of his brothers and presented them to Pharaoh. Pharaoh asked Jacob how old he was. Jacob told him that he was 130 years old. Then Jacob blessed Pharaoh.

Joseph took his father and brothers to Goshen where there was a great abundance of grass for their herds. In Goshen, the sons of Jacob raised their families and their flocks. The Israelites, the descendants of Israel (Jacob), were fruitful and greatly increased in number.

The Death of Jacob

Jacob lived in Egypt for seventeen years. Then he fell ill. When Joseph heard of his father's illness, he rushed to his bedside with his sons Ephraim and Manasses. When Jacob saw his grandsons, he blessed them.

Then Jacob called together all his sons and told them that one day, God would lead them back to Canaan. He told them that he wished to be buried, not in Egypt, but in Canaan. Then he blessed them all and prophesied what would become of each of them and of their families. Then Jacob died.

Joseph threw himself onto his father's face weeping and kissing him. Then he

ordered his doctors to embalm the body. After Joseph and his brothers had mourned for seventy days, they, along with a large group of people, carried Jacob's body back to Canaan. In accordance with his wishes, they buried Jacob in a cave. Then Joseph, his brothers, and the rest of the people returned to Egypt.

The Death of Joseph

Joseph lived to be 110 years old. He lived to see his grandchildren, great-grandchildren, and great-great-grandchildren. When Joseph realized that he was dying, he called his brothers to him. He told them that they would have trouble, but that God would surely come to their aid and lead them to the land that He had promised to Abraham, Isaac, and Jacob. Joseph told them to take his bones with them when they left. With that, he died. His body was embalmed and placed in a coffin.

Chapter Review — Fill in the blanks to complete the sentences below.

1. To test his brothers, Joseph had his _silver cup_ placed in Benjamin's sack.

2. When Joseph threatened Benjamin, _Judah_ offered himself as a slave in Benjamin's place.

3. In Egypt, Jacob and his sons settled in _Goshen_.

4. The _Israelites_ were the descendents of Jacob.

Chapter 9

The Patience of Job

Tragedy Befalls Job

God Blesses Job

During the time of Abraham, Isaac, and Jacob, there was a good and holy man who lived in what is now Saudi Arabia. God had blessed him with seven sons and three daughters. He also had thousands of sheep, camel, oxen, and donkeys. In addition, he had many servants who worked for him. Yet, it was not only for his great wealth that people loved him, but also for his great goodness and faithfulness to God's laws.

One day, Satan came before God. God asked him what he had been doing. Satan replied that he had been walking around the Earth. God asked Satan if, during his walk, he had seen Job, who was the holiest man on Earth. Satan said that he had seen Job but that it was not hard for Job to love and serve God because God had blessed Job so greatly. Satan said that if God allowed harm to befall Job, then Job would curse the Lord. God responded that Satan might bring harm to Job but that he could not harm Job's body.

Tragedy Befalls Job

Soon after this, Job was having dinner. A messenger burst into the room to tell Job that some bandits had taken his oxen and his donkeys and killed the servants tending them. The first messenger had hardly finished speaking when a second messenger rushed into the room. He told Job that fire had fallen from heaven and burned up all Job's sheep and the shepherds watching them. He alone had escaped to deliver the message. Then a third courier charged into the room. He said that the Chaldeans had attacked Job's herd of camels, stolen them, and killed the servants watching the camels. Yet, the saddest news still awaited Job.

The third messenger had barely finished his report when a fourth servant burst into Job's house. He told Job that while his sons and daughters ate dinner at their oldest brother's home, a terrible wind had blown down the house. The house had collapsed on the young people. They had all been killed.

When Job heard this last terrible news, he stood up and tore his clothes. Yet, he fell to the ground and adored God. "The Lord gave, and the Lord has taken away. Blessed be the name of the Lord," he prayed. Job did not blame God for all these terrible disasters and God was pleased.

Satan Attacks Job's Body

Again Satan appeared before God. God pointed out that Job had not cursed Him despite the evil that Satan had done to him. However, Satan replied that Job had not *really* suffered. If God allowed Satan to harm Job's body, then Job would curse the Lord. So God told Satan that he could physically harm Job but that he could not kill him.

Satan caused Job to contract a wretched disease. Horrible sores appeared all over his body. Job had to scrape his sores with a piece of broken pottery. Job's wife, seeing his miserable condition, criticized him! She told him that he should curse God and die. Yet Job rebuked her. He told her that God had given them many good things, should they not then receive the bad that God allowed as well? Thus Job did not sin against the Lord.

Job's Wife Criticizes Him

When Job's friends heard what had happened to him, three of them came to comfort him. Seeing his ravaged body, they cried and wept. His friends sat down and for the next week no one spoke as they saw that Job was in terrible pain.

Finally, Job spoke and cried about his awful suffering. His friends replied by blaming him for his disease! They said that he must have done something terrible for God to punish him like this. Job told his friends that they had done a poor job in comforting him. Job also maintained his innocence and the goodness of God.

God Rewards Job's Faith

Finally, God rewarded Job's steadfast faith in Him. God restored all that Job had lost two times over. Once again, Job was blessed with seven sons and three daughters. He lived 140 more years. He saw his children's children to the fourth generation. When Job died, he was an old man. God had filled his life with great joys and blessings.

Job's Friends Blame Him

Chapter Review

Fill in the blanks to complete the sentences below.

1. Job lived in <u>Saudi Arabia</u>.

2. Job's children were killed when <u>they were at their oldest brothers home.</u> <u>the house where they were eating fell on them</u>

3. Whom did Job's friends blame for his disease? <u>Job</u>

4. How did God reward Job's faith? <u>He restored all that Job had lost two times over</u>

Let My People Go: Moses

Pharaoh's Daughter Finds Moses

The Birth of Moses

In time, Joseph and his brothers died, but the Israelites (the descendents of Israel) had many children. They quickly became a large part of the population of Egypt. At the same time, new Pharaohs, who did not know Joseph, came to power. These Pharaohs feared the power of the Israelites so they began to oppress them. They turned the Israelites into slaves and forced them to build great cities in Egypt.

In spite of their hard lives, the Israelites, or Hebrews as they were also called, continued to prosper and have many children. Finally, the Pharaoh issued a most terrible and evil command. He ordered all the male babies born to Hebrew women to be thrown into the Nile River where they would drown.

A particular Hebrew woman gave birth to a son. Of course, like any mother, she loved him very much. For three months, she hid her son from the Egyptians. Finally, finding that it was no longer possible to keep him hidden, she placed him in a papyrus basket and coated it with tar so that it would float. Then she put her beloved son into the basket and placed it among the reeds along the Nile River's bank. She sent her daughter, the boy's sister, to watch the basket to see what would happen.

Before long, Pharaoh's daughter came down to the Nile to bathe. She saw the basket floating in the reeds and sent her maid to retrieve it. When Pharaoh's daughter opened the basket, she saw the baby and knew it was one of the Hebrew boys. The little baby was crying and she felt sorry for him.

At that moment, the baby's sister came out of her hiding place. She asked Pharaoh's daughter if she would like her to find a Hebrew woman who could nurse the baby.

Pharaoh's daughter told her to find such a woman. So the girl went and got the baby's own mother. Pharaoh's daughter gave her the baby to nurse. When he had grown older, she returned him to Pharaoh's daughter. She adopted him and he became her son. She named him Moses, which means "saved from the waters."

Moses Flees from Egypt

One day when Moses had become a grown man, he went out to where his own people, the Hebrews, labored. He saw an Egyptian beating a Hebrew slave. When no one was looking, Moses killed the Egyptian and hid his body. Yet, the Pharaoh learned

Moses Kills an Egyptian

of his deed. He decided to kill Moses. However, Moses fled to Midian, in Arabia.

Arriving in Midian, Moses sat down at a well to rest. While he was resting, some women brought their sheep to the well. Other shepherds tried to drive the women away, but Moses came to their rescue. In time, Moses fell in love with one of the girls and married her. Moses lived in Midian for forty years tending the flocks of Jethro, his father-in-law.

Meanwhile, in Egypt, the Pharaoh died, but the Israelites continued to toil in slavery. They begged God for a deliverer. God heard their prayers and answered them.

God Calls Moses to Save His People

One day when Moses had led his sheep to the Mount of Horeb, God appeared to him in a burning bush. Moses saw that though the bush was on fire, it did not burn up. Moses was curious and decided to see what the burning bush meant.

As Moses approached the bush, God called out to him. God told Moses to remove his sandals because he was standing on sacred ground. When Moses heard the voice of God, he fell on the ground and hid his face because he was afraid to look at God.

God told Moses that He had seen the misery and heard the cries of the Hebrews in Egypt. God explained to Moses that He had chosen him to lead His people out of the land of their suffering to a land flowing with milk and honey. At first, Moses

many miracles for them. When they had seen and heard God's message, they believed Moses and adored God.

The Ten Plagues of Egypt

Moses and Aaron then went before Pharaoh and demanded that he let the Hebrews go into the wilderness and sacrifice to God. However, Pharaoh refused. In fact, he ordered that the Hebrews be given no straw to make bricks. They would have to gather straw in the evening to make bricks, thus making their lives even more miserable.

God commanded Moses to return to Pharaoh. This time, at God's command, Aaron threw his staff in front of Pharaoh. The staff immediately became a snake. Pharaoh summoned his sorcerers and they threw their staffs down as well. They also became snakes but Aaron's snake swallowed their snakes. Pharaoh hardened his heart and would not let the Hebrews leave.

The next morning, Moses confronted Pharaoh on the banks of the Nile. Again Moses demanded the release of the Hebrews. Again Pharaoh said no. Then God commanded Aaron to stretch his staff over the Nile River. Aaron thrust his staff into the river and all the waters of Egypt turned to blood. All the fish died and the water stank terribly. The Egyptians could not drink the water of the Nile. They had to dig along the Nile to find water to drink. Yet Pharaoh still refused to allow the Hebrews to leave.

After seven days, Aaron again stretched out his hand over the Nile. This time frogs came and covered the land.

objected. He said that he was a weak man who did not speak well. Yet, God promised that He would be with Moses and told him that Aaron, his brother, would be his spokesman. So Moses agreed to return to Egypt to deliver the Hebrews from slavery.

Moses Returns to Egypt

Moses returned to Egypt. Along the way, God sent his brother Aaron to meet him. Together, they assembled the Hebrew leaders. Moses and Aaron told them what God had said to Moses and performed

The First Plague:
The Rivers of Egypt Turn to Blood

Still Pharaoh's heart was hard. Then the Lord turned the dust of the ground into flies and insects that stung both men and animals. Next God sent a plague on the Egyptian cattle. All the Egyptian cattle died, but cattle owned by the Hebrews stayed healthy. Then the Egyptians suffered from a plague of boils.

The seventh plague was hail. Thunder, lightning, and hail destroyed crops, trees, and homes. It was the worst storm in the history of Egypt. The only place spared was Goshen where the Hebrews lived. Still Pharaoh would not let the Hebrews leave.

The eighth plague was locusts. What little had not been destroyed by the hail, was eaten by the locusts which covered the land. Then an impenetrable darkness covered the land. Yet, Pharaoh's heart was hardened. He told Moses never to appear before him again. Pharaoh told Moses that if he saw him again, he would kill him.

Chapter Review

Fill in the blanks to complete the sentences below.

1. Where did Pharaoh's daughter find Moses? *The nile river*

2. "Moses" means *"saved from the waters"*

3. Moses fled from Egypt because he *killed a man*

4. God spoke to Moses from a *burning bush*.

5. *Aaron* was Moses' brother.

6. The first plague turned all the rivers of Egypt into *blood*.

The Israelites Leave Egypt: Moses

The Passover Meal

The Passover Meal

Now God told Moses that He would send one final plague. After that, Pharaoh would release the Hebrews. Yet, before God sent the final plague, He wanted the Israelites to be prepared for it. Therefore, Moses and Aaron commanded each family to prepare a lamb that had no defects. On the fourteenth of the month, the family was to sacrifice the lamb and take some of the blood and spread it on the sides and the tops of the doorframes of their homes.

God also commanded that the lamb be roasted along with bitter herbs and eaten with unleavened bread. The people were to eat the meal as though they were about to leave on a journey. They were to have their cloaks tucked into their belts, they were to be wearing their sandals, and their staffs should be in their hands. The Israelites did as the Lord commanded.

The Tenth Plague: the Angel of Death

In the middle of the night, an angel came through Egypt and killed the first born of every Egyptian family. From Pharaoh's first-born, to the first-born of the lowliest prisoner in Pharaoh's dungeon, the angel of death spared no family. Yet, the angel, seeing the blood on the doorposts of the Israelites, *passed over* their homes and spared their children. All over Egypt, there was wailing, for there was not an Egyptian home without someone dead.

When Pharaoh saw the dead, he called Moses and Aaron to see him. He *demanded* that they take the Hebrews and leave Egypt. The Egyptian people also urged the Israelites to leave because they were afraid every Egyptian would die if they stayed.

Thus, many generations after Jacob came into Egypt, his descendants left. About 600,000 men, not counting women and children, began the journey out of Egypt. With them, the Israelites carried the bones of Joseph.

The Parting of the Red Sea

God led the Israelites out of the land of their slavery. During the day, God appeared as a pillar of cloud. At night, He appeared as a pillar of fire. Thus, day and night, God guided the Israelites. Finally, after several days of traveling, the Israelites arrived at the Red Sea.

Meanwhile, back in Egypt, Pharaoh had changed his mind about letting the Hebrews leave. He ordered his generals to call out the army to pursue and re-capture them. He took six hundred of his best chariots and charged after the Israelites.

When the Israelites saw the Egyptian army surging toward them from behind and the Red Sea in front of them, they were very afraid. Yet Moses encouraged them and promised them that the Lord would fight for them. They needed to do nothing.

The cloud that had been leading the Israelites went behind them and created a protective wall between them and the Egyptian army. On the Egyptian side, it was dark, but on the Hebrew side it was light. Thus, the two forces were separated during the night.

God commanded Moses to stretch out his staff over the Red Sea. The sea parted, creating a wall of water on each side and a dry path down the middle. During the night, the Hebrews passed down the dry path to the bank on the far side. In the morning, the Egyptians, seeing the path, tried to follow. However, God commanded Moses to stretch forth his staff once again. This time the water returned to its place. Pharaoh and the entire Egyptian army were drowned. Not one of them survived.

The Israelites in the Desert

From the Red Sea, Moses led the Israelites to the Desert of Shur. For three days, they traveled in the desert but were unable to find water. When they finally did find a well, it was too bitter to drink. However, Moses performed a miracle and made the water drinkable.

After being in the desert for six weeks, the Hebrews could not find enough food. They began to complain about Moses and wished that they had stayed in Egypt where there was plenty of food. God promised that He would rain bread down from Heaven every morning. Each evening, a huge number of quails flew into the Hebrew camp where they were easily caught. In the morning, the ground was covered with thin flakes like frost. The Israelites did not know what the flakes were. They cried out "Man hu?" that is, "What is this?" Moses told them that it was the bread that the Lord had promised them. They were commanded to take only as much as they needed for one day. They did and found that the flakes tasted like fine flour mixed with honey.

Some people took more of the flakes than they needed for one day. The next morning, their "manna" had gone bad. Moses was angry with these people for disobeying God.

(For forty years, God fed the Hebrews with manna from Heaven. When they arrived in Canaan, the manna fell no more.)

Some time after the first fall of manna, the people began to run low on water. Again they complained to Moses.

God told Moses to take his staff and strike a rock. He did as God commanded and immediately water began to flow from the rock. The people drank their fill and quenched their thirst.

The Defeat of the Amalekites

While the Israelites were in the desert, the Amalekites attacked them. Moses told Joshua, his military commander, to choose some men to fight the Amalekites. Joshua

did as Moses ordered. During the battle, Moses stood on top of a nearby mountain with his hands raised. As long as his hands remained lifted, the Hebrews pushed back the Amalekites. However, when Moses tired and his hands fell, the Amalekites had the better of the battle. Finally, Aaron and another man named Hur held up Moses arms. By the end of the day, Joshua had defeated the Amalekites.

The Chosen People

Three months after their departure from Egypt, the Israelites arrived at Mount Sinai. God called Moses up to the top of the mountain. Here God spoke to Moses. God told Moses to remind the Israelites of how much He had done for them and how much more He would do for them as long as they stayed obedient. God told Moses to return to the people and instruct them to be consecrated to God as His "Chosen People."

When Moses descended the mountain, he told the people what God had said. They agreed to do as the Lord had asked. Then God told the people to bathe and wash their clothes for the next two days and to be ready for the third day. On the morning of the third day, there was thunder and lightning on the top of Mount Sinai. A thick cloud covered the mountain. The top of the mountain was on fire and the mountain shook. Then came the sound of a mighty trumpet that became louder and louder. Everyone in the Hebrew camp was afraid and trembled. Then Moses led everyone out of the camp and stood at the foot of Mount Sinai.

Chapter Review

Fill in the blanks to complete the sentences below.

1. There were _ten_ plagues.

2. What was the Last Plague? _the angel of death_

3. When God led the Israelites out of Egypt, He appeared as a pillar of _cloud_ during the day and a pillar of _fire_ at night.

4. The Egyptian army drowned in _the Red Sea_.

5. To sustain the Israelites in the desert, God sent _quails_ in the evening and _manna_ each morning.

6. _Joshua_ commanded the Israelite army.

Chapter 12

The Ten Commandments: Moses

The Ten Commandments

God descended to the top of Mount Sinai and called Moses to him. There God spoke to Moses. He said

1. I am the Lord thy God. Thou shall not have any strange gods before Me.
2. The Name of God is holy. Thou shall not take the name of the Lord thy God in vain.
3. Remember to keep holy the Lord's Day.
4. Honor thy father and thy mother.
5. Thou shall not kill.
6. Thou shall not commit adultery.
7. Thou shall not steal.
8. Thou shall not bear false witness against thy neighbor.
9. Thou shall not covet thy neighbor's wife.
10. Thou shall not covet thy neighbor's goods.

When Moses came down from the mountain, he built an altar and offered a sacrifice to God. He took the blood of the sacrifice and sprinkled it on the heads of the people as a sign of the covenant that God had made with the people that day. Then Moses returned to the top of Mount Sinai with Joshua.

For forty days and nights, Moses stayed on Mount Sinai speaking with God. The Lord gave him two stone tablets on which He had written the Ten Commandments. While Moses was on the mountain, down in the Hebrew camp, the people grew restless.

The Ten Commandments

The Golden Calf

The people went to Aaron and asked him to make them a "god" like those of the Egyptians to lead them. They did not know what had happened to Moses but were unwilling to wait any longer for his return. So Aaron told them to bring him all the gold earrings of their wives and daughters.

Aaron was a weak man so when they brought him the gold, he did not have the strength to resist their evil demand. So he took the gold, melted it down, and crafted it into a golden calf. Then the people built an altar and placed the calf idol upon it. The Hebrews gathered around the altar and made sacrifices to the golden calf. Then

they began to eat and drink. They became drunk and began to behave like pagans.

On Mount Sinai, God told Moses what the Israelites were doing. God was very angry and threatened to destroy the people for whom He had done so much. Moses begged God not to destroy the people. God relented and did not bring disaster down upon the Chosen People. Moses turned and went down the mountain carrying the two stone tablets upon which God had written the Ten Commandments.

When Moses came down from the mountain and saw the Israelites behaving like pagans he was extremely angry. He

threw down the two stone tablets on which the Ten Commandments were written, breaking them. He seized the gold calf and threw it into the fire. Then Moses ground the calf into powder, put it into water, and made the Israelites drink it.

Turning to Aaron, Moses demanded why he had created the calf. Weakly, Aaron could only blame the others. Then Moses called the sons of Levi to him. He told them to go through the camp and kill all the idolaters that they found. Many thousands of men were slain on that day.

The next day, Moses told the people that they had committed a great sin against God. He said that he would go back up Mount Sinai and beg God for His forgiveness.

Moses returned to the peak of Sinai and prayed that God would forgive the Hebrews. The Lord heard his prayer. God told Moses to cut two new stone tablets like the ones he had broken. Upon these tablets, God again wrote the Ten Commandments. When God had finished speaking with Moses, he came down from the mountain with the two tablets.

While on the mountain, God had let Moses see His back. As a result, Moses' face shone like the sun. When the people saw his face, they were afraid of him and dared not speak to him. Yet Moses told them not to be afraid. From then on, Moses wore a veil over his face when he spoke to the people.

Hebrew Law

Up to this point, the Hebrews had no set place where they could worship God. Neither did they have any guidelines for the worship of God. Therefore, besides the Ten Commandments, God also gave Moses other rules that he wished the Israelites to follow. These rules had to do with public worship of Him. Moses told the Hebrew people exactly what God wanted them to do in order to build a place of worship and the manner in which He wished them to worship Him.

The Tabernacle

First, God instructed Moses to have the Israelites build a **tabernacle**. This was a tent built according to very specific requirements. The people covered the tent in precious gems, gold, and rich cloth. Inside the tabernacle hung an incredible tapestry that divided the tabernacle into two parts. The smaller part of the tabernacle was called the **Holy of Holies**. The larger part was called the **Sanctuary**.

Inside the Holy of Holies, Moses placed the **Ark of the Covenant**. The Ark was a small box made of the most expensive wood and covered in gold. Two solid gold cherubim (angels) were mounted on top of the box at either end. The cherubim, which faced each other, had their wings spread toward each other, overshadowing the cover. Inside the Ark, Moses placed the Israelites' most holy relics: the two tablets upon which God had written the Ten Commandments.

Inside the Sanctuary were three objects consecrated to God's worship. The first object was a table. The second was a candlestick made of pure gold. The candlestick had seven candleholders. The candles were to burn all night. Lastly, there was an Altar of Incense upon which the finest incense was burned.

Around the tabernacle, Moses had the Israelites build a courtyard. Inside the courtyard were two other sacred objects. The first was the **Altar of Burnt Offerings**. This is where the Hebrew priests sacrificed their burnt offerings. The second object was the **Bronze Basin**, which the priests used to purify themselves before they offered the sacrifice.

[These Hebrew rules have relevance to Catholics today. The Ark represents the tabernacle in Catholic Churches. Instead of the tablets, today the Holy Eucharist is kept inside the tabernacle. The Holy of Holies has become the altar on which the Catholic priest offers the sacrifice of the Mass. The Hebrew Sanctuary is the sanctuary of today's Catholic church. It is the place that the priests occupy during the Sacrifice of the Mass. The courtyard represents the body of the church where the people now worship. The seven-branched candlestick has become a red candle that burns day and night to show that Our Lord is truly present in the tabernacle.

Under Hebrew Law, sacrifices were either bloody or unbloody. In the bloody sacrifices, the Hebrews offered sheep, goats, and doves to God. They offered cakes, unleavened bread, and wine in the unbloody sacrifice. Again, these have Catholic relevance. The bloody sacrifices prefigured the bloody sacrifice of Christ upon the cross. The unbloody sacrifices were a type of Sacrifice of the Mass.]

Chapter Review

Fill in the blanks to complete the sentences below.

1. God called Moses to _Mount Sinai_, where He gave him the Ten Commandments.

2. _Honor thy father and thy mother_ is the Fourth Commandment.

3. "Thou shall not steal" is the _Seventh Commandment_.

4. While Moses was away, the people pressured Aaron to create a _golden calf_.

5. The Jewish Tabernacle was divided into the _Holy of Holies_ and the _Sanctuary_.

6. The _Ark of the Covenant_ contained the two tablets upon which were written the Ten Commandments.

7. What is kept inside the tabernacle of a Catholic Church? _What is kept inside the tabernacle of a Catholic Church is the Holy Eucarast._

44

Chapter 13   An Ungrateful People: Moses

The Hebrew Religious Feasts

In addition to His Laws and the Ten Commandments, God also created a number of religious feasts for the Israelites. The first feast was the **Feast of Unleavened Bread** or **Passover** or the **Paschal** feast. During Passover, the Israelites were to eat a lamb and for seven days eat unleavened bread. This was to remind them of their deliverance from Egypt.

The next feast was **Pentecost**. It was celebrated seven weeks after Passover. Pentecost was celebrated to remember the time when God gave Moses the Ten Commandments on the top of Mount Sinai. During this feast, God required the Israelites to give Him a donation of the first fruits of the harvest.

The third feast was the **Feast of Tabernacles**. This feast served to remind the Hebrews of their long trek in the desert. During this feast, the Lord required that the Israelites live in tents made from tree branches.

The fourth feast was the **Feast of Expiation** also known as the **Day of Atonement** ("**Yom Kippur**" in Hebrew). During this feast, the priest sacrificed a young cow to atone for his sins and a young goat to atone for the sins of all the other people. Then the priest entered the Holy of Holies carrying a golden censor and the blood of the victims. He would incense the Ark and sprinkle the blood on the ground. (Yom Kippur remains the most solemn holiday for Jews today.)

The Ministers of Divine Worship

In addition to the creation of the holy feasts, God also created a priesthood for the Israelites. The leader of the priests was the **High Priest**. The first high priest was Moses' brother Aaron. Moses consecrated Aaron High Priest, anointed him, and clothed him in the vestments of his office. Under Aaron were the **Priests**. The priests were the sons of Aaron. It was their job to offer the sacrifices. The **Levites** were the lowest order of the Hebrew priesthood. These men all belong to the tribe of Levi, the same tribe as Moses and Aaron. Their job was to care for the Tabernacle.

The Mission to the Promised Land

The Israelites remained camped at Mount Sinai for one year. Then the Lord told Moses to send some men to explore the land of Canaan, which God had promised to the Israelites. Moses chose twelve of the leading Israelites for this important mission to explore the Promised Land. Joshua and Caleb were among the men he sent.

Aaron Was the First High Priest

The People Complain about Moses

When the people heard the explorers' report, they were very sad. Many wept because they felt that Moses had led them astray. The people began to speak against Moses and Aaron. They began to wish that they had remained in Egypt or had died in the desert. Joshua and Caleb told the people that Canaan was a wonderful place that the Lord would give to them if they remained obedient to Him. Still the people complained and grumbled. They even talked of stoning Moses and returning to Egypt.

When the complaining reached its peak, God told Moses to deliver a message to the people. For all their complaining and wickedness, He would punish them. No one over the age of twenty would be allowed to enter the Promised Land. Only Joshua and Caleb, who remained loyal, would be exempt. For forty years, the Israelites would wander in the desert.

The Revolt Against Moses

Some time later, two hundred fifty of the leading Israelites rebelled against Moses and Aaron and denied their authority. Three men -- Korah, Dathan, and Abiram -- led the rebellion. The next day, God commanded the people not to go near these wicked men. While the Israelites looked on, the ground opened under the feet of the rebel leaders and swallowed them, their families, their tents, and all their property. Then a fire came down from Heaven and consumed the other two hundred fifty mutineers. From then on, no one questioned the authority of Moses.

After forty days, the men returned with their report. They also brought back samples of the various fruits that grew in Canaan. Two of the men carried a massive bunch of grapes that hung between them from a pole they carried on their shoulders. The men reported that the land did indeed flow with milk and honey. However, they said that the people who lived in Canaan were giants. The men warned Moses not to attack the Canaanites because they were stronger than the Israelites.

Moses Doubts God

While wandering in the desert, the Israelites ran out of water. Once again, they began to complain. God told Moses to speak to a nearby rock and it would yield water. Moses picked up his staff, and for a moment he doubted. Instead of just speaking, he struck the rock twice with his staff. Water poured forth in great abundance. Yet, because Moses doubted, and struck the rock, he displeased God. God told Moses that because he had not believed, he would not be allowed to lead the people into the Promised Land.

A short time after this, Aaron died. His son Eleazar became High Priest.

The Bronze Serpent

Some time later, the Israelites again ran out of water and began to complain that they had neither food nor water. In punishment, God sent poisonous snakes among the people. The snakes bit the people, many of whom died from the agonizing poison.

The people came to Moses and begged for God's forgiveness. They pleaded for Moses to pray to God to take away the snakes. So Moses prayed for the people.

God commanded Moses to make a bronze serpent and set it up on a pole as a sign. He did so. Anyone who looked at the serpent was healed.

The Death of Moses

Moses had lived a long and holy life. Yet all men are mortal and must die. When the time came for Moses to die, the Lord commanded him to speak to the Israelites. Moses told them that he was 120 years old. He explained to

MOSES STRIKING THE ROCK

them that God had told him that he would not cross the Jordan into the Promised Land with them. Moses placed his hands upon Joshua and told the people that from now on, Joshua would be their leader.

Then Moses reminded the people of all the things that God had done for them. He commanded them always to love and obey the Lord and His commandments. Moses told Joshua to be strong and courageous and to remember that God would always be with Joshua and would never abandon him.

When Moses had finished speaking, he climbed from the plains of Moab to the top of Mount Nebo. There, God showed him Canaan. The sight of Canaan filled Moses with joy and he rejoiced. Full of happiness and gratitude, Moses died. God buried him in a valley in Moab. For thirty days, the Israelites remained on the plains of Moab mourning their leader. Moses had been the greatest of the Old Testament prophets.

Chapter Review

Fill in the blanks to complete the sentences below.

1. The Jewish feast of _Passover_ was to remind the Jews of their deliverance from Egypt.

2. The feast of _Pentecost_ was celebrated to remember the time when God gave Moses the Ten Commandments on the top of Mount Sinai.

3. The _Levites_ were the lowest order of the Hebrew priesthood. Their job was to care for _the Tabernacle_.

4. For all their complaining and wickedness, the Lord caused the Jews to wander in the desert for _forty_ years.

5. Why was Moses not allowed to enter the Promised Land? _Moses was not allowed to enter the Promised Land because Moses doubted God._

Chapter 14 — The Walls Come Tumbling Down: Joshua

The Priests Carry the Ark of the Covenant

The Israelites Enter the Promised Land

After the death of Moses, God commanded Joshua to cross the Jordan River into Canaan. God promised Joshua that He would be with him. The people obeyed Joshua as they had Moses.

Joshua sent two spies to explore Canaan. Joshua was especially interested in the city of Jericho, which was strongly defended by high walls. When the spies explored Jericho, a woman there hid them. In exchange for her help, the spies promised that when the Israelites captured the city, that she and her family would not be harmed. Then the spies returned to Joshua. They told him that the people of Jericho feared the Israelites.

Early in the morning, Joshua ordered his people to cross the Jordan River. The priests took the Ark of the Covenant and marched before the people. When the priests carrying the Ark came to the banks of the River Jordan, the water upstream stopped flowing. The water downstream continued to flow. This created a dry path that allowed the people to pass. When all the Israelites had crossed to the other side of the Jordan, the river returned to its normal course. The people camped neared Jericho, where they praised the Lord for his goodness.

The Walls of Jericho Come Down

Jericho was a big city with a large population. Strong, high walls fortified it. God gave Joshua specific instructions for capturing Jericho. Joshua and his soldiers marched around the city one time, each day, for six days. Seven priests, carrying trumpets, marched in front of the Ark of the Covenant. On the seventh day, Joshua and his soldiers walked around the city seven times. The seven priests blew their trumpets and the people all shouted. At the sound of the shouting and the trumpets, the walls of the city crumbled.

The Israelites charged into Jericho. They slew every living person and animal in the city. They spared only the woman who had helped them and her family. They burned the city and everything in it.

The Hebrews Receive the Promised Land

In time, under Joshua's command, the Israelites conquered all of Canaan just as God had promised them. They divided the land among the twelve tribes of Israel. Each tribe was descended from one of the twelve sons of Jacob, and bore the name of that son. Thus, after many years of

wandering, the Israelites had been given the land that God had promised to them.

Joshua lived to be 110 years old before he died. While he lived, the Israelites obeyed God and did His will. The generation after Joshua also obeyed God, but after them the people began to disobey God. The Israelites, who owed everything to the Lord, were an ungrateful people. Sadly, their pagan neighbors easily led them astray. They began to worship idols like the pagans. In punishment for their sins, God no longer helped them. When the Israelites went into battle, the hand of God was against them and their enemies defeated them.

The Judges

Under the rod of their enemies, the Israelites turned to God, repented, and declared their dependence on him. Having repented and humbled themselves before Him, God had mercy on them. He sent fifteen holy men and one woman called *Judges*, selected from the Israelites, to deliver them and to rule over them.

As long as the Judge lived, the Israelites remained repentant. Yet when each Judge died, the Israelites returned to their old sin of idolatry. For four hundred years, the Israelites switched back and forth. First they worshiped God, then idols -- repenting and relapsing.

Of the sixteen Judges sent during this time, the greatest were Gideon, Samson, and Samuel. The one woman Judge was Deborah. Under Deborah's leadership the Hebrews won a great victory over the Canaanites who had oppressed them for twenty years.

Chapter Review

Fill in the blanks to complete the sentences below.

1. After the death of Moses, _Joshua_ became the leader of the Israelites.

2. The walls of _Jericho_ fell before the trumpets and shouting of the Israelites.

3. The twelve tribes of Israel descended from each of the twelve sons of _Jacob_.

4. The greatest Judges were _Gideon_, _Samson_, and _Samuel_.

5. _Deborah_ was the only woman Judge.

The Horn of Gideon

God Calls Gideon to Be His Judge

Following a relapse into idolatry, God gave the Israelites into the hands of the Midianites for seven years. Whenever the Israelites planted their crops, the Midianites invaded the country. They destroyed the crops and killed all the livestock. The Midianites so impoverished the Israelites that they cried out to God for help. When the Israelites cried out, God sent them a Judge. His name was Gideon.

The Sword of Gideon

One day, God appeared to Gideon who was threshing wheat in a winepress to keep it from the Midianites. God told Gideon to go forth to save Israel. However, Gideon did not feel that he was the right man for the task. God assured Gideon that He would help him strike down the Midianites.

The Lord told Gideon to tear down the altar to the pagan statue, Baal, which the Israelites were worshiping and make a sacrifice to the one, true God. Gideon did as he was told. However, as he feared the townspeople, he acted at night. In the morning, the people of the town woke up and saw Baal's altar demolished. They asked who had destroyed the altar. When they learned it was Gideon, they demanded he be killed. Gideon told those gathered, who demanded his death, that anyone who fought for Baal's statue would be dead by morning. He told them that if the statue of Baal were really a god he could fight for himself.

Gideon Defeats the Midianites

Now all the Midianites and their allies crossed over the Jordan and camped in the Valley of Jezreel. God told Gideon to summon the Israelites for a battle. Gideon sent messengers to gather the people, calling them to arms.

Early in the morning, Gideon and all his men camped at the spring of Harod. The Lord told Gideon that he had too many men in his army. If they won the battle, the Israelites would think it was because of their own strength. So God told Gideon to tell anyone who was afraid to go home. Twenty-two thousand men left, but ten thousand remained.

Yet again the Lord told Gideon that he had too many men. God told Gideon to take the men down to the spring and have them drink. So Gideon took the men down to the water. There, God told Gideon that only those men who drank water from their cupped hands, rather than lapping the water like dogs, would be part of the army. Only three hundred drank from their cupped hands. God told Gideon that with these three hundred men He would deliver the Midianites into Gideon's hands.

During the night, Gideon divided his men into three units. He gave them each a trumpet and a jar with a torch inside. "Watch me," he told them. "When I get to the edge of the enemy camp, do exactly as I do. When I blow my trumpet, then from all around the camp, blow yours and shout, 'For the Lord and for Gideon.'"

Gideon and the hundred men with him reached the edge of the enemy camp. They blew their trumpets and broke the jars that they held. The other men also blew the trumpets and smashed their jars. Grasping the torches and blowing their trumpets, they shouted, "A sword for the Lord and for Gideon!" When the three hundred trumpets sounded, God caused the Midianites in the camp to turn on each other with their swords. Those Midianites who were not killed cried out as they fled.

After Gideon's great victory, the Israelites asked Gideon to be their king. Gideon told them that he would not rule over them for the Lord would rule them. During Gideon's life, the Israelites were at peace and worshiped the true God. Sadly, as soon as Gideon died, the Israelites again began to worship the statue of Baal. For their idolatry, the Lord delivered them into the hands of the Philistines for forty years.

Chapter Review

Fill in the blanks to complete the sentences below.

1. Gideon tore down the altar of __Baal__.

2. Gideon defeated the __Midianites__.

3. Before the battle, Gideon gave each of his men a __trumpet__ and a __jar with a torch inside__.

Chapter 16

The Strongest Judge: Samson

Samson Slays a Vicious Young Lion

Again the Lord sent a Judge to the Israelites. His name was Samson.

Samson's Marriage

When Samson was a young man, he saw a young Philistine woman. When he returned home, he told his father and mother that he wanted to marry her. Samson's wish upset his parents because the Philistines were oppressive rulers. Still, Samson was determined. His parents did not know that his wish to marry her came from God, Who was seeking an occasion to confront the Philistines.

As Samson was on his way to meet the Philistine woman, a young lion suddenly came roaring toward him. The Spirit of the Lord came powerfully upon him so that he tore the lion apart with his bare hands. He told no one what he had done. He continued into town to talk with the woman whom he liked very much.

Some time later, when Samson went back to marry her, he stopped to look at the lion's dead body. In it, he saw that a swarm of bees had made a honeycomb. He scooped out the honey with his hands and ate it as he walked. When he rejoined his parents, he gave them some honey, which they ate. He did not tell them where he had found the honey.

After his wedding, Samson held a feast that thirty Philistine men attended. At the feast, Samson made a wager with the men about a riddle. Samson bet them that if they solved the riddle in seven days, he would give them each a fine suit of clothes. If they did not solve it, they each had to give him a fine suit of clothes. They agreed. Samson told them the riddle:

"Out of the eater, came meat; out of the strong, came sweet."

For three days, the Philistines tried, but could not solve the riddle. On the fourth day, they threatened to kill Samson's wife and her family if she did not tell them the answer to the riddle. Samson's wife threw herself on him crying that he did not love her because he had not told her the answer to the riddle. She continued to cry and moan until on the seventh day, he finally told her. She then explained the riddle to her people.

Before the end of the seventh day, the men of the town explained the riddle to Samson:

"What is sweeter than honey? What is stronger than a lion?"

They had solved the riddle but Samson knew it was his wife who had told them. Furious, the Spirit of the Lord came powerfully upon him. He killed thirty Philistines, stripped them of their garments, and gave their clothes to those who had explained the riddle. Burning with anger, he returned to his father's home.

Samson's Vengeance

Later on, Samson went to visit his wife but her father would not let him in the house. He told Samson that he had allowed her to go away with another man. This filled Samson with anger. He went out and caught three hundred foxes and tied torches to their tails. He lit the torches and let the foxes loose in the cornfields of the Philistines. The foxes burned up the corn, the vineyards, and olive groves.

When the Philistines learned who had destroyed their fields and grain, they killed Samson's wife and her father. Samson promised the Philistines that for these murders, he would punish them. He attacked them viciously and slaughtered many of them. Another time he slaughtered one thousand Philistines with the jawbone of a donkey.

Samson and Delilah

Some time later, Samson fell in love with an evil Philistine woman named

like tissue paper. The secret of his strength was not discovered.

Delilah was very upset. She accused Samson of lying to her. Again, she demanded that he tell her the secret of his strength. He said that if he were tied with new ropes that he would become as weak as any other man. So Delilah took new ropes and tied him with them. Then, with men hidden in the room, she called to him, "Samson, the Philistines are upon you!" He snapped the ropes as if they were threads.

Delilah continued to nag and pester Samson. Day after day, she prodded him to tell her his secret until he was sick to death of it. So finally he told her everything. "No razor has ever been used on my head," he said. "If my head were shaved, my strength would leave me, and I would become as weak as any other man." When Delilah saw that he had told her everything, she sent word to the rulers of the Philistines to come to her home. The rulers of the Philistines returned with her money. After Samson fell asleep, she called for someone to shave off his hair. Then she called, "Samson, the Philistines are upon you!"

Delilah. The Philistine rulers went to her and asked her if she could find out how Samson came by his great strength. They knew if they could discover his secret that they could make him their prisoner. They promised her a great deal of money if she helped them.

So Delilah asked Samson to tell her the secret of his great strength. Samson answered that if he were tied with seven fresh bowstrings that he would be as weak as any other man. The rulers of the Philistines brought her seven fresh bowstrings and she tied him with them. With men hidden in the room, she called to him, "Samson, the Philistines are upon you!" Laughing, he snapped the bowstrings

Samson awoke from his sleep ready to kill the Philistines, but he did not know that the Lord had left him. The Philistines seized Samson, blinded him, and took him down to Gaza. They made Samson grind grain in the prison. Over time, they failed to notice that hair on his head began to grow back.

The Death of Samson

idol, Dagon. They shouted that Samson be brought out so that they could make fun of him. They dragged Samson out of the prison and humiliated him. Samson asked the slave who guided him to lead him to the pillars that supported the temple, so that he could lean against them.

Philistine men and women filled the temple. All the rulers of the Philistines were there. On the temple roof, about three thousand men and women watched the feast. As he leaned against the pillar, Samson prayed to God. He asked God to give him strength one last time. Then Samson grabbed the two central pillars that supported the temple. Bracing himself against them with one hand on each pillar, Samson said, "Let me die with the Philistines!" Then he pushed with all his might. The temple crashed down on the rulers and all the people in it. Thus Samson killed many more when he died than while he lived.

To celebrate Samson's capture, the Philistines assembled for a luxurious feast as well as to offer a great sacrifice to their

Chapter Review

Fill in the blanks to complete the sentences below.

1. Samson's great enemies were the _Philistines_.

2. What fierce animal did Samson kill with his bare hands? _a young lion_

3. One time, Samson caught _300 foxes_, tied torches to their tails, lit the torches, and let them loose in the cornfields of his enemies.

4. Samson killed _one thousand_ _Philistines_ with the jawbone of a donkey.

5. Samson finally told the secret of his strength to _Delilah_.

6. Samson died when he _made the temple to come crashing down_ _how? by pushed the two main pillars._

Judge and High Priest: Samuel

God Calls Samuel

One of the last Judges was Eli, who was also the High Priest. During his time as Judge, there lived a holy couple named Elkanah and Hannah. Hannah had no children, which made her very sad. One day, she went to pray at the temple and begged God to give her a son. She promised that if she had a son, she would consecrate him to God. God answered her prayer. She named her son Samuel.

When Samuel was about three years old, Hannah took him to the High Priest, Eli. Eli consecrated Samuel to God. Samuel remained in the temple to serve God. As Samuel grew older, he also grew in holiness.

One night, as Samuel slept, God called to him. Samuel, thinking Eli called him, rose and went to Eli. Yet Eli told him that he had not summoned him and to return to sleep. This happened three times before Eli realized that it was God Who was calling Samuel. Eli told Samuel that the next time he heard someone calling

Samuel is Presented to Eli

him, he should say, "Speak, Lord, for your servant is listening." This Samuel did.

The next morning, Eli called Samuel. Samuel told Eli all that God had said to him. Samuel let Eli know that God was going to punish him and his two sons. God was punishing the sons because they were evil men who had committed blasphemy. Eli was being punished because he had not punished his sons for their sins. When Eli heard what Samuel said, he accepted the Will of God.

Some time after God spoke to Samuel, a bloody war broke out between the Philistines and the Israelites. In the first battle with the Philistines, the Philistines defeated the Israelites and killed many of them. In the next battle, the Israelites carried the Ark of the Covenant before them, thinking that God would help them. Yet God was not with the Israelites. The Philistines killed thirty thousand of them, including Eli's two sons. The Philistines also captured the Ark. When Eli, who was ninety-eight, heard the news of his sons' deaths and the loss of the Ark, he fell off the chair upon which he sat, broke his neck, and died. He had led Israel for forty years.

Samuel Becomes Judge

The Philistines took the Ark of the Covenant to the temple of their "god," the statue Dagon. The next day the statue of Dagon had fallen on its face in front of the Ark. The Philistines stood the statue of Dagon back up, but the next day it had fallen again. This time the statue had broken into pieces. God sent other afflictions on the Philistines. Mice overran their fields and pestilence ravaged the cities. Finally the people demanded that the Ark be returned to the Israelites. The Ark, along with a sum of gold, was returned to the Israelites.

After the death of Eli, Samuel became the High Priest and Judge of Israel. He assembled the people and pointed out that they had sinned against God. He promised that if they repented, God would deliver them from the hands of the Philistines. The people fasted and confessed. When the Philistines attacked, God was with the Israelites and gave them victory over their enemies. The Philistines were defeated and stopped invading the Israelites lands. For many years, peace reigned over the land. Samuel ruled Israel the rest of his life.

Ruth

During the time of the Judges, a man named Elimelech went with his wife, Naomi, and their two sons to the land of Moab. In Moab, the sons found women to marry. Sadly, after about ten years, Elimelech and his two sons died. Overcome with grief, Naomi decided to return to Bethlehem. Her two daughters-in-law said that they would accompany her.

After the three women had traveled for a while, Naomi tried to persuade her daughters-in-law to return to their own land where they had family. One of the women returned, but the other, Ruth, would not. She went with Naomi to Bethlehem. The two women arrived in Bethlehem at harvest time.

Since they were poor, Ruth had to work in the fields picking up stray stalks of wheat that had been missed by the reapers. A man named Boaz, who was related to Elimelech, owned the field in which she worked. During the day, Boaz came to the fields to oversee the reapers. When he saw Ruth and heard of her courage and faithfulness to Naomi, he spoke kindly to her. He told her not to collect wheat in any other field but his. Boaz said that he had spoken to his workers and that they would not bother her as she collected the wheat. Moreover, if she became thirsty, she could go to the water jugs from which his workers drank. Boaz also told his reapers to drop some wheat on purpose so that Ruth could more easily collect it.

As time went on, Boaz and Ruth began to spend time together. Eventually, they fell in love and married. God blessed them with a son whom they named Obed. Obed was the grandfather of David. It was from this family that Jesus descended.

Boaz Makes Sure that Ruth Finds Plenty of Wheat

Chapter Review

Fill in the blanks to complete the sentences below.

1. When Samuel was three years old, his mother, *Hannah*, took him to the High Priest, *Eli*, who consecrated him to God.

2. How did the Philistines obtain the Ark of the Covenant? *in a bloody war*

3. Where did they put the Ark? *In front of their god Dagon in the Temple of Dagon*

4. Why did they return the Ark? *God sent disasters because when our their god's statue into*

5. Ruth married *Boaz*.

A King in Israel: David

King Saul

When Samuel became old, he appointed his sons Judges over Israel. However, they did not follow his, or God's, ways. They were dishonest and corrupt. So the leaders of Israel came to Samuel and asked him to appoint a king, like other nations had, to lead Israel.

When Samuel heard that the people wanted a king, he was very angry. He felt that the only king Israel should have was God Himself Who had done so much for the Israelites. God spoke to Samuel and told him that the people could have a king if they wished. However, God also told Samuel to warn the people that a king would treat them harshly. In fact, one day they would cry out to God to deliver them from their king. When that day came, God said He would not answer. Despite this warning, the people refused to listen to Samuel.

Samuel Meets Saul

In a short time, Samuel anointed Saul King of Israel. Saul, who came from the tribe of Benjamin, was thirty years old. Saul was a courageous man who was highly respected by the people. He was also tall and very good-looking.

At the beginning of Saul's reign, God was with him. With God's help, Saul defeated his enemies. However, there came a time when Saul's greed got the better of him and he disobeyed God's orders.

Saul's Disobedience

Samuel told Saul that it was God's wish that the Amalekites be destroyed for making war upon the Israelites. Saul was to attack the Amalekites and kill them all as well as all of their flocks and herds. Saul did attack the Amalekites but he spared their king and the best of their flocks. On his return, Saul built a monument to commemorate his victory. For his disobedience, Samuel told Saul that the Lord regretted making him King of Israel. This was the last time that Samuel ever spoke to Saul although he prayed for Saul.

David Is Chosen king

The Lord ordered Samuel to go to Bethlehem, to the house of Jesse, because He had chosen another to be King of Israel. When Samuel arrived in Bethlehem, David, Jesse's youngest son was in the meadow, tending his father's sheep. Samuel sent for him and anointed him with oil. As God's Spirit came upon David, He left Saul.

David and Saul

When the Spirit of the Lord left Saul, he became deeply depressed. When Saul fell into fits of depression, his servants suggested that someone who could play the harp be found to play for Saul to brighten his mood. When Saul learned that David was a fine harp player, he sent for him. David entered Saul's service.

Saul liked David very much. In fact, David became one of Saul's armor bearers. Whenever Saul fell into a depression, David would play the harp for him and he would feel better. However, Saul did not know that David had been consecrated king.

David and Goliath

A new war soon broke out between the Israelites and their old enemies the Philistines. The Philistine army camped on one mountain and Saul and the Israelites camped directly across from them on another. In between the two camps lay a narrow valley.

One morning, a gigantic Philistine named Goliath came out of their camp. He was almost ten feet tall. Goliath wore a bronze helmet on his head, a coat of heavy chain mail armor, and bronze greaves on his legs. He carried a huge spear whose iron point weighed fifteen pounds. His shield bearer walked before him.

He stood at the edge of the Philistine camp and shouted across the valley to the Israelites. He challenged them to send their best man to fight him. For forty days, he issued his challenge. Yet no one in the Israelite camp had the courage to accept the challenge.

One day, Jesse sent David to the camp to see how his brothers, who were in the army, were doing. David arrived in the camp and ran to the battle lines to ask his brothers how they fared. As he talked with them, Goliath shouted his usual challenge. When David saw Goliath and heard his taunts, David was furious. He asked the men around him why no one had accepted the challenge. Word reached Saul of David's words, so Saul sent for him. David told Saul that he would fight Goliath.

At first, Saul refused David because he was only a boy while Goliath was a seasoned warrior. Yet David told Saul that when lions and bears attacked his father's flocks, he had fought and defeated them. God had saved him from the claws of the lion and the jaws of the bear; He would save him from Goliath. So, Saul agreed to let David fight the giant.

Saul dressed David in his own armor and gave David his own sword. David tried to walk around in the armor but, not being used to it, could not. So he removed it. Instead, he took his shepherd's staff and went to a nearby stream where he chose five smooth stones, which he put into his bag. Thus, armed with only his sling, he went to meet the Philistine giant.

When Goliath saw that David was little more than a boy, he despised him and threatened him. Yet David was not afraid because God was with him. As Goliath strode closer to him, David reached in his bag for one of the stones. He slung it and struck Goliath on the forehead with such force that the stone sank into his forehead, killing him. Goliath pitched forward onto his face. David ran forward and stood over the gigantic body. He drew Goliath's massive sword from its sheath and cut off Goliath's head.

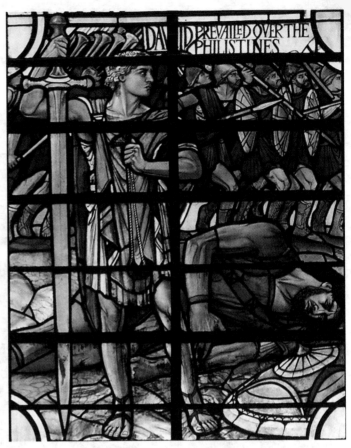

David Slays Goliath

When the Philistines saw that their great champion had been slain, they fled in panic. The Israelites surged forward with shouts of joy and charged after their fleeing enemy. The Israelites killed many of them. Then the victorious army returned and pillaged the Philistine camp.

Chapter Review

Fill in the blanks to complete the sentences below.

1. _Saul_ was the first King of Israel.

2. _Samuel_ warned the Jews that one day a king would oppress them.

3. When Saul fell into depression, David would play the _harp_ for him.

4. David killed _Goliath_ with only his sling and a stone.

Chapter 19

Saul's Jealousy and Hatred: David

Saul Was Angry When He Heard the Women Praise David (Note Saul's face)

Saul's Hatred for David

When Saul and his army returned from their victory over the Philistines, the women of Israel came out to greet them. The women were singing and dancing. As they danced, they sung that Saul had killed the Philistines by the thousands, but David had killed them by the ten thousands. When Saul heard this song, he was very angry.

The next day, Saul was in a very bad mood. He called David to play the harp for him. Saul grabbed a spear and threw it at David, but David evaded the spear.

Shortly after this, Saul gave David command of a thousand soldiers whom David successfully led in a number of campaigns. This caused the Israelites to love David more and more. However, it caused Saul to hate him even more deeply.

One day, Saul offered to let David marry his daughter if David killed two hundred Philistines. Saul hoped that the Philistines would kill David. Yet David killed the

Philistines, which caused the people's love of David to increase. When Saul saw how the people loved David, his hatred grew and he determined to kill David.

Jonathan's Love for David

As much as Saul hated David, Saul's son, Jonathan, loved David. They often spoke of Saul's hatred for David. When Saul told Jonathan that he planned to kill David, Jonathan told David to go into hiding. Jonathan spoke with his father about all that David had done against the Philistines and convinced him not to kill David. For the time being, Saul was appeased and David returned.

Saul Tries to Kill David

Once more war broke out with the Philistines. For a fourth time, David went to war against the Israelites' old enemy. David won a shattering victory over them. Yet, his victory only caused Saul new and greater anger and jealousy.

One day as David played his harp for Saul, Saul seized a spear and tried to pin David to the wall with it. Yet David was quick and agile and evaded the thrust. Saul drove the spear into the wall and David escaped once again. Jonathan tried to talk to his father to make him understand that David was not his enemy. Yet Saul was beyond reason. He grabbed his spear and in his rage threatened his own son. When Jonathan saw this, he knew that Saul meant to kill David.

Jonathan met David in a field and told him what had happened. Jonathan warned him and advised him to flee. The two friends wept when they realized that this was the last time that they might see each other. Jonathan promised David that he and their descendents would be friends forever. Then David fled into the hills and Jonathan returned home.

Saul Tries to Kill David

Saul Hunts David

For a while, David was in constant danger from Saul who hunted for him. Yet David put his life into the hands of God Who protected him.

One time, Saul pursued David with three thousand soldiers. Tired after the chase, Saul entered a cave in which David had hidden with his small band of men. Of course, Saul did not know that David lay concealed in the cave. David's men wished to kill Saul, but David would not allow it. Instead, he cut a piece of cloth from Saul's robe to let Saul know he had been there.

Another time, Saul and his army were chasing David when David quietly crept into Saul's camp while everyone slept. David's companion would have killed Saul in his sleep, but again David spared his life. David merely took the spear that stood by Saul's bed.

When David was some distance outside of Saul's camp, he called down to Saul and his men. When Saul awoke, he saw that David had taken his spear. He knew that David could have easily killed him if he had wanted to do so, but had spared his life. Saul was filled with remorse and repented of his actions against David. Saul returned home with his army and David went on his way.

The Death of Samuel

In the meantime, Samuel died. All of Israel assembled. They mourned him and buried him at his home.

The Death of Saul

Once again, war broke out between the Israelites and the Philistines. King Saul assembled the Hebrew army and marched forth to meet his mortal enemies. The Philistines fought hard and forced the Israelites to flee before them. The Philistines were in hot pursuit of Saul and Jonathan. They caught and killed Jonathan. Soon, the fighting grew fierce around Saul. When the Philistine archers overtook him, they critically wounded him. Fearing that he would fall into the hands of his enemies, Saul fell on his own sword.

Saul's sinful suicide freed David from danger. Yet, David did not rejoice. He recalled Saul's virtues and the times when Saul had been a good and noble king. He also wept bitterly at the death of his best friend Jonathan.

Chapter Review

Fill in the blanks to complete the sentences below.

1. After David's victory over Goliath, Saul tried to kill David with a _Spear_.

2. Saul's son, _Jonathan_, and David were best friends.

3. David had a few chances to kill King Saul but instead he only took _a spear_ and _a piece of cloth_

4. How did King Saul die? _King Saul died by falling on his sword (suicide)._

Chapter 20

Israel's Greatest King: David

David Becomes King of Israel

After Saul's death, David became King of Israel. David conquered Jerusalem and made that city his capital and his residence. When the Philistines learned that David was king of Israel, they launched an attack on him. With God's help, David utterly defeated the Philistines. In addition to the Philistines, during his reign as king, David defeated many other enemies. His many victories brought great treasure into Jerusalem.

The Ark of the Covenant Is Placed on Mount Zion

David was not only a great war leader. He was also concerned with spreading, by his example and influence, the worship of the one true God. On Mount Zion in Jerusalem, he built an incredible tent in which to place the Ark of the Covenant. When everything in the tent was ready, David and all the people carried the Ark in a procession to the tent. Three thousand soldiers acted as the honor guard for the Ark. The princes of Israel dressed in their richest purple robes while the priests dressed in white. In the procession, the people played harps, lyres, cymbals, and trumpets. David himself walked before the priests playing his harp and dancing. Every few feet, the priests sacrificed a bull and a young cow to God.

David Walks Before the Priests Playing His Harp and Dancing

David's Justice

David realized that any good king must provide his subjects with justice. Thus, David was concerned that his people be treated fairly. He chose wise men for his counselors and honest men to help rule the people. He appointed honest men to manage and oversee the royal treasury and the royal lands. During King David's reign, there was order and justice throughout the land.

When King David died, he left a kingdom that was larger, wealthier, and more well administered than when he became king. The Israelites would look upon David's reign as the high point in their history. David would be considered the greatest of their kings.

David's Sins

David was a great king and a holy man, yet he committed two grievous sins for which the Lord punished him. Both sins involved a woman named Bathsheba.

One evening, David got up from his bed and walked around on the roof of his palace. From the roof, he saw a very beautiful woman bathing. David sent a servant to find out who she was. The servant said her name was Bathsheba. She was the wife of Uriah the Hittite, a soldier in David's army. Then David sent other servants to bring her to his palace. She came to the palace and they committed adultery. Then she went back home. In order to cover this sin, David committed a second terrible sin.

In the morning, David wrote a letter to Uriah's commander, Joab. In the letter, David told Joab to "put Uriah out in front where the fighting is fiercest. Then withdraw from him so he will be struck down and die." Joab followed David's order, and Uriah was killed in battle. After Uriah's death, David married Bathsheba and they had a son. Of course, God was very displeased with David.

God sent the prophet Nathan to David. Nathan fearlessly told David that he had committed serious sins. David admitted that he had sinned and confessed his sins. Nathan replied that God forgave David but for his sins, God was going to punish him.

David Looks on from his Roof as his Servant Talks to Bathsheba

Absalom's Revolt

David's punishment came from his son Absalom. Absalom was an ambitious man who wanted to seize his father's throne. Absalom began his revolt by traveling around Israel, making promises to many of its people. When he thought that enough people supported him, he openly revolted against his father, King David. People from all over the kingdom flocked to join Absalom.

A messenger came to David and told him that the hearts of the people of Israel were with Absalom. David warned the officials who were with him in Jerusalem that they had to flee, or none of them would escape from Absalom. David fled from Jerusalem to the Mount of Olives, weeping as he went. Absalom gathered his army and pursued his father.

When the two armies met in battle, David's soldiers defeated Absalom's army. Absalom fled. However, in his haste, he failed to notice that he was riding under a large oak tree. Absalom's long thick hair got caught in the low hanging branches of the oak tree. Absalom was left hanging in midair, while the mule he was riding kept on going.

When Joab, David's commanding general, heard that Absalom was hanging in the tree, he ran to the tree. David had told his men not to harm his son. Despite David's orders, Joab thrust three spears into the ungrateful heart of the traitor. Joab threw Absalom's body into a deep pit and piled a large stack of rocks on top of it.

The news of his son's death filled David with sorrow. Weeping bitterly, he cried out: "Absalom my son, would to God that I might die for thee." After this, David returned to Jerusalem with his army. Huge crowds of people came out to greet him on his return.

The Death of David

When David was seventy years old, he realized that he was nearing the end of his life. He called together the princes and the leading men of the kingdom. He told them that he had always wanted to build a Temple to God. He explained that he had gathered all the materials to build a magnificent Temple, but that God had forbidden him to build the Temple because he was a man of war and blood. Thus, it would fall to his son, Solomon, to build the Temple. God would allow Solomon to build the Temple.

Before he died, David gave Solomon very detailed instructions as to how to build the Temple. He reminded Solomon that the Temple was to be the dwelling place for the Lord. David told Solomon to keep God's laws and commands so that he would prosper in all that he did. David advised Solomon to serve the Lord with a gentle heart. If he did these things, God would never forsake him.

When David died, he had ruled Israel for forty years. He was buried in Jerusalem. Solomon, his son, became king.

David Speaks to Solomon about the Temple

Chapter Review

Fill in the blanks to complete the sentences below.

1. When David became king, he conquered _Jerusalem_ and made that city his capital and his residence.

2. King David built a magnificent tent on Mount Zion in which he placed _the Ark of the Covenant_.

3. David had _Bathsheba's husband Uriah_ killed.

4. David's son, _Absalom_, led a revolt against him.

5. God had forbidden David to build the Temple because _he was a man of war and blood_.

6. When David died his son, _Solomon_, became king.

The Wisdom of Solomon

Chapter 21

Solomon Prepares to Build the Temple

God Grants Solomon Great Wisdom

At the beginning of his reign, Solomon took David's counsel to heart. He obeyed God's rules and commands. As a result, the Lord blessed him.

One night, God appeared to Solomon in a dream. God told Solomon that He would grant Solomon anything that he requested. Solomon asked for a discerning heart to govern the people and to distinguish between right and wrong. The Lord was pleased that Solomon had asked for wisdom instead of long life, wealth, or the death of his enemies. Therefore, God gave what Solomon had asked: wisdom. In addition, God gave him what he had not asked for: riches, honor, and a long life.

In addition to wisdom, God gave Solomon a great breadth of knowledge and a very keen insight. He understood the nature of creation, geology, chemistry, physics, and astronomy. He had an incredible knowledge of plant life and the medicinal properties of the various plants. He also had a remarkable knowledge of animals, birds, reptiles, and fish. Soon, news of Solomon's great wisdom and knowledge spread all over the world. Kings, who had heard of him, sent envoys to listen to Solomon.

A Wise Ruling

One day, two women came before Solomon demanding that he decide their case. The first woman explained that the two of them lived together in the same house. She had a baby and three days later, the second woman also had a baby. During the night, the second woman's son died. So she got up in the middle of the night and took the first woman's son from her side while she slept. The second woman put the dead boy in place of her son. The next morning, the first woman got up to feed her son, but he was dead! However, when she looked at him closely in the morning light, she saw that it was not her son.

Then the other woman spoke up: "No! The living one is my son; the dead one is yours." Still the first one insisted, "No! The dead one is yours; the living one is mine." Thus they argued before King Solomon.

Then Solomon said, "Bring me a sword." His soldiers brought him a sword. Then he gave an order: "Cut the living child in two and give half to one woman and half to the other."

Solomon Makes a Wise Decision

When the mother of the living child heard this order, she was filled with love for her son. In agony, she cried out to Solomon, "Please, my lord, give her the living baby! Don't kill him!" Yet the other woman said, "Cut him in two!" Then Solomon gave his ruling: "Give the living baby to the first woman for she is his mother."

Soon all of Israel knew of Solomon's verdict. The people were in awe of Solomon because they saw that he had wisdom from God to administer justice.

Solomon Builds the Temple

In his fourth year as king, Solomon began construction on the Temple in Jerusalem. This massive project required almost two hundred thousand men to build the incredibly huge and magnificent Temple. For the exterior of the Temple, Solomon used only the finest stone and wood. He had the interior walls covered in gold. Masons crafted fantastic carvings of angels, trees, and flowers. Nothing in the history of the world had been created to rival it.

After seven years, the Temple was finished. Solomon assembled the people of Israel. The priests carried the Ark of the Covenant from Mount Zion to the sanctuary that he had prepared for it in the Temple. The people paraded before the Ark while the priests played harps, cymbals, and trumpets. All the people sang praises to God. As the people processed, they stopped frequently to offer sacrifices of sheep and oxen to the Lord.

Solomon Dedicates the Temple to God

When the priests placed the Ark within the sanctuary, a cloud filled the Temple. The people fell to their knees praising God, for He was in the cloud. Then Solomon, standing before God's altar, lifted up his hands to Heaven. He dedicated the Temple to God and gave thanks for all that the Lord had done for the people of Israel. When Solomon finished his prayer of dedication, he and all of Israel offered sacrifices to the Lord.

God later appeared to Solomon and told him that He had heard his prayers and had consecrated the Temple. The Temple that Solomon had built would be a place where God would dwell. God also promised that as long as Solomon and his descendents obeyed the Lord, that He would always ensure that his descendents would sit on the throne of Israel.

The Glory of Solomon

For the first twenty years of his reign, Solomon adhered to the counsel that his father David had given him. As a result, God gave Solomon innumerable blessings. Solomon's wisdom and greatness were known far and wide. Nations paid him tribute. He built a fleet of merchant ships that sailed over the known world, bringing gold into his treasury.

With the money he had, Solomon built many cities throughout Israel. He improved Jerusalem until it was a magnificent city. He also constructed an incredibly beautiful palace, the walls of which he lined with gold.

During these years, Israel enjoyed peace. Solomon had a strong army, so his neighbors sought his friendship and his advice. One of his most wealthy neighbors was the Queen of Sheba. When she heard of his fame and his wisdom, she came to test him.

The Queen of Sheba arrived in Jerusalem with a large caravan full of gold, spices, and precious gems. She tested Solomon with difficult questions. However, he answered them all easily. When she saw his wisdom, his magnificent palace, and the glorious Temple, she was overwhelmed.

The Fall of Solomon

Regrettably, Solomon's reign did not end as it began. As he became older, some of his wives who were pagans led him away from God. He became corrupted and even turned to idolatry. The man, who had built the magnificent Temple to the Lord, built temples to idols to please his wives. This made the Lord very angry.

As punishment for his sins, God told Solomon that He would divide the kingdom of Israel. However, because of the love that God had for David, He promised not to divide the kingdom while Solomon lived. The kingdom would be taken from his son. His son would rule only a portion of the once great kingdom.

Thus Solomon fell from greatness. He began to oppress his people until revolts sprang up all about him. When Solomon died, his son Rehoboam became king. Solomon had ruled for forty years.

Chapter Review

Fill in the blanks to complete the sentences below.

1. Solomon asked God for _Wisdom_ instead of long life, wealth, or the death of his enemies.

2. The Queen of _Sheba_ was one of the rulers impressed with King Solomon's wisdom.

3. Why did King Solomon build pagan temples? _He built pagan temples to please his wives._

4. As punishment for his sins, God told Solomon that _He would divide the kingdom of Israel._

Fire from Heaven: Elijah

God Sends a Prophet to Condemn King Jeroboam for Worshiping Idols

The Division of the Kingdom

Following Solomon's death, the leaders of the people came to Rehoboam and asked him to lighten the burden that Solomon had placed on them in his later years. Rehoboam told them to return in three days. During the three days, he consulted with his advisors. The older advisors told him to lighten the people's load. Foolishly, Rehoboam rejected this counsel. Instead, he went to his younger advisors who told him to treat the people even more harshly than his father had. This was the advice that Rehoboam decided to follow. On the third day, he met with the leaders of the people. He told them that he would make their yoke even heavier than that which they already bore.

When the people heard Rehoboam's message, they became very angry and stoned his messenger. Then they made Jeroboam, one of Solomon's advisors, their king. Only the tribes of Judah and Benjamin remained loyal to Rehoboam. Thus, as God had promised Solomon, the kingdom of Israel was divided into two parts: Israel and Judah. Jerusalem remained the capital of Judah. Later, Samaria became the capital of Israel.

Jeroboam Leads His People into Idolatry

Soon after the kingdom divided, Jeroboam began to fear that if his subjects went to the Temple in Jerusalem to worship, they would became part of the kingdom of Judah and not return to him. Thus, he told them that the journey to Jerusalem was too far. He told them that he would provide them with gods to worship. So, he made two golden calves for his people to worship. Sadly, the people listened to him and worshiped the false gods.

The Decline of the Israelites

For two hundred fifty-three years, Israel and Judah remained separate kingdoms. During this time, Israel had nineteen kings. Most of them came to power through violence and murder. They were evil men who engaged in various sins, especially idolatry. During their reigns, the people lived lives of vice.

To punish the kings and show the people the correct path, God sent holy men called prophets to the people of Israel. These prophets preached and performed miracles both in Israel and in Judah.

In addition to sending prophets, God also punished the Israelites by allowing them to suffer at the hands of their enemies. Regrettably, the Israelites were a stubborn people who would not listen to the prophets nor obey God. Thus, they brought punishment upon themselves.

The Prophet Elijah

Of all the wicked men to rule Israel, perhaps the most evil ruler was King Ahab. He married an immoral pagan woman named Jezebel. Together they built a temple to a pagan god called Baal and appointed 450 priests to serve this "god." At the same time, Ahab murdered all the priests of the true God that he could find in Israel.

Ahab did more to offend the Lord than all the other kings who went before him. As a result, God sent Elijah the prophet to announce a great drought. He told Ahab

An Angel Feeds Elijah

that no rain would fall in Israel. Ahab was furious! He tried to kill Elijah. However, God protected Elijah. He told Elijah to hide in a ravine by the Jordan River. There, God sent angels to feed Elijah.

Each morning and evening, angels brought Elijah food. He drank from the brook near where he hid. In time, the brook dried up. So God told Elijah to go to Zarephath in the region of Sidon, where a widow would feed him.

Elijah and the Widow of Zarephath

Following God's command, Elijah went to Zarephath. As he entered the city he met the widow of whom God had spoken. She was gathering some sticks. He asked her for a drink of water. As she was getting his water, Elijah also asked her for a piece of bread. She answered that she did not have any bread. She had only a small bit of flour and a little oil in a jar. She was gathering the wood to make one last meal for herself and her son. After they had eaten that meal, they would die.

Elijah told her not to be afraid but to go and make him a small loaf of bread and something for herself and her son. He promised that there would be flour and oil until God sent rain. The woman did as Elijah told her and as he had promised there was always flour and oil in her home.

Some time later, the widow's son became ill and died. Elijah took the boy into his arms and went into his room to pray. He asked God to restore the boy to life. God answered Elijah's prayers. When the woman

saw that God had restored her son, she knew that Elijah was truly a man of God.

Elijah and the Priests of Baal

For three years, no rain fell in Israel. Then God told Elijah to go see Ahab and He would send rain to the land. Elijah did as God had commanded. When Ahab saw Elijah, he was very angry. Ahab said that Elijah was to blame for all the problems plaguing Israel. Yet, Elijah said that it was Ahab himself who was the cause of the problems because of his many sins, especially his worship of the idol of Baal.

Then Elijah told Ahab to summon the people of Israel and all the priests of Baal to meet him on Mount Carmel. When the people, the priests, and King Ahab were all assembled, Elijah spoke to them. Elijah proposed a test to see whether Baal or the Lord was the true God.

Elijah said that he and the priests of Baal would each build an altar. Upon the altar, they would each place a dead bull. Under the bull, they would place wood, but not light the wood. Then Elijah would call upon God and the priests of Baal would call upon Baal to send down fire to burn up the bull. The god who answered by fire was the real God. This proposal greatly pleased all the people.

Then the priests of Baal prepared themselves. They called upon Baal to send fire to burn up their bull. For hours, they screamed and danced but nothing happened. After several hours, Elijah began to laugh at them. He taunted them saying that they needed to scream louder because Baal was asleep or busy or on a trip and could not hear them. The priests of Baal screamed even louder and began to cut themselves with knives and swords. Still, Baal did not speak. By evening, they finally gave up.

Then Elijah called the people to come to him. He dug a trench around his altar and filled it with water. Next Elijah poured gallons of water on the wood and the bull. The wood under the dead bull was soaked. The ground around the altar was soaked and the trench was filled with water. Then Elijah prayed to God to show His power so that the people might believe. When Elijah finished praying, a great fire came down from Heaven. The bull, the wood, the water, and even the stones of the altar, were completely burned up.

The great crowd that had gathered fell down on their knees. They began to pray to the one true God. Elijah ordered that the priests of Baal be captured and killed. Then the Lord kept His promise and sent rain to Israel.

God Answers Elijah

Chapter Review

Fill in the blanks to complete the sentences below.

1. Under King Rehoboam, the kingdom of Israel was divided into _Israel_ and _Judah_.

2. God sent the prophet Elijah to chastise King _Ahab_ and Queen _Jezebel_.

3. Elijah challenged the priests of _Baal_ to a test. Elijah and the priests each placed a _bull_ upon an altar. The true God would send _fire_ from Heaven.

The Justice of God: Elisha

The Just Punishments of Ahab and Jezebel

Idolatry was just one of the many sins that Ahab and Jezebel committed. They also were greedy murderers. It was for their murder of a man named Naboth that God finally gave them their just punishment.

Naboth owned a vineyard near King Ahab's palace. Ahab wanted the vineyard and offered to buy it from Naboth. However, the vineyard had been in Naboth's family for a very long time so he refused to sell it to Ahab. This made Ahab and Jezebel very angry. Jezebel had false witnesses accuse Naboth of cursing God and the king. As a result, Naboth was stoned to death, and Ahab and Jezebel took his vineyard.

God commanded Elijah to go to Ahab and Jezebel and tell them that for their crime they would die horrible deaths. Three years later, this prophecy was fulfilled. Ahab was killed in battle and dogs licked up his blood. Some time after this, Jezebel was thrown out of a window and trampled to death by horses.

Elijah Is Taken to Heaven in a Fiery Chariot

As Elijah grew old, the Lord commanded him to take Elisha as his successor. When the time came for God to take Elijah to Heaven, Elijah told Elisha to leave him. However, Elisha refused to go. He told Elijah that he would not leave him. As the two prophets walked along, a chariot of fire drawn by horses of fire appeared from Heaven. Elijah was taken up to Heaven by a whirlwind in the fiery chariot. Elisha watched until Elijah was gone. Then he picked up Elijah's cloak and put it upon his own shoulders. Suddenly, the spirit and powers of Elijah filled Elisha.

Elijah Is Taken to Heaven in a Fiery Chariot

Elisha and the Gang of Thugs

Some time later, Elisha was walking to the city of Bethel when a gang of young thugs who lived in the city insulted him. Elisha called upon the name of the Lord and two bears rushed from the nearby woods. The bears attacked the gang members and killed forty-two of these wicked youths.

Elisha and the Shunammite Woman

One day, Elisha was traveling in Shunem. There a generous woman asked him to come into her home for some food. As Elisha often passed her home in his travels, she asked her husband to build a small room for Elisha so that he could spend the night at their home. After spending several nights at the Shunammite woman's home, Elisha told her that for her kindness to him, God would bless her with a son. The following year, she did have a baby boy just as Elisha had promised.

Tragically, when the boy was about eight years old, he unexpectedly became ill and died. The Shunammite woman ran to find Elisha and begged him to come and help her son. Elisha entered the room where the dead child lay upon his bed. Elisha prayed that the Lord might restore the lad to life. God answered the prophet's prayers. Elisha called the Shunammite woman who hugged her living son.

Elisha and Naaman

On another occasion, Naaman, a famous Syrian general, came to Elisha to ask him to cure his leprosy. When Naaman arrived at the house where Elisha was staying, Elisha sent out his servant instead of speaking to Naaman himself. The servant instructed Naaman to go to the Jordan River and wash himself seven times and he would be cured. However, Naaman was furious. He was a very important man and not used to being treated this way. He left because he thought that Elisha had slighted him by not coming out and personally curing him.

However, Naaman's servants spoke to him to calm him down. They told him that Elisha had instructed him in the means to a cure. As a result, Naaman did go to the Jordan River and bathed in it seven times. He was cured as Elisha had promised.

Naaman returned to Elisha and proclaimed that there was indeed no god but the God of Israel. Naaman then offered to give Elisha a gift for helping him, but Elisha refused all his offers. So Naaman left.

After Naaman was gone, Elisha's servant, Gehazi, ran after Naaman. Gehazi thought that he would take a gift from Naaman. When Gehazi caught up to Naaman's chariot, Gehazi told him that Elisha had sent him for some silver and two changes of clothes. Naaman gave him the money and the clothes.

When Elisha next saw Gehazi, he asked him where he had been. Gehazi said that he had not been anywhere. Elisha told Gehazi that he knew he was lying. He told Gehazi that his spirit had been with Gehazi as he had gone to Naaman's chariot. Elisha told Gehazi that as punishment for his sin, the leprosy that had been Naaman's would cling to Gehazi and his children. Gehazi left covered in leprosy.

Elisha's Last Miracle

Elisha lived many years and performed many miracles. Finally he became sick and died. Some time after his death, another man died and his friends sought to bury him near Elisha's grave. Suddenly, a band of marauders fell upon them. The bandits threw the dead man's body into Elisha's grave. The dead man had barely touched Elisha's body, when he sprang to life and stood on his feet. Thus did God do miracles among the Jewish people through the relics of His saints.

Elisha Tells Gehazi that He Knows He is Lying

Chapter Review   Fill in the blanks to complete the sentences below.

1. Ahab and Jezebel murdered _Naboth_ to steal his vineyard.

2. Elijah was taken up to Heaven in _fiery chariot_.

3. Elisha cured _Naaman_, a famous Syrian general, of _his leprosy_.

4. What was Elisha's last miracle? _Elisha's last miracle was a gang of bandits fell upon people who were burying a man and the bandits threw the man into Elisha's grave and he was restored to life._

Chapter 24

In the Belly of the Beast: Jonah

Jonah Is Thrown into the Sea

After the death of Elisha, God chose a good and holy man named Jonah to be His prophet. One day, God told Jonah to go to the city of Nineveh. The people of Nineveh were evil and had committed many sins. Jonah was afraid to go to Nineveh. He thought the men there would harm him. So Jonah decided not to go to Nineveh. He boarded a ship going in the opposite direction from Nineveh.

After Jonah had been sailing for one day, God sent a violent storm. Thunder and lightning filled the air. Fierce wind and huge waves rocked the ship upon which Jonah sailed. The storm was so fierce that the sailors feared the ship would sink. The captain ordered everyone to pray that they be saved. Finally they cast lots, asking God to indicate who was the cause of the storm. They drew Jonah's name.

Jonah told the captain of the ship who he was. He told the captain that he had disobeyed God. Jonah told the captain to throw him overboard if he wanted to save his ship. The sailors, who were good men, did not want to throw him overboard. They knew he would drown in the rough seas. However, the storm became worse and worse. Asking God's forgiveness, they threw Jonah into the sea.

As soon as Jonah hit the water, the storm stopped. Jonah did not drown. Instead, a great whale came and swallowed him in one gulp. For three days and nights, Jonah lived in the belly of the whale. He prayed for God's forgiveness.

On the fourth day, the whale spit Jonah out onto the beach. Once again Jonah heard the voice of the Lord commanding him to go to Nineveh. Jonah fully realized that he could not escape God. He left the beach and began to walk to the city.

The Whale Spits Jonah onto the Beach

In Nineveh, Jonah began to preach to the people. He told them that unless they stopped their evil ways that God would severely punish them. Wisely, the people listened to Jonah. They began to pray for mercy and abandoned their wicked behavior.

God saw what the people of Nineveh were doing. He saw that they had given up their sinful lives. Thus, the Lord changed His mind and did not punish them.

Chapter Review

Fill in the blanks to complete the sentences below.

1. God told Jonah to go to the city of *Nineveh*.

2. Jonah spent three days in *the belly of a whale*.

Chapter 25

An Angel for a Companion: Tobias

Tobit and Anna

In the days before the birth of Our Lord, there lived a man named Tobit. When he became old enough, he married a woman he loved named Anna. Tobit and Anna had a son whom they named Tobias. Later Tobit and Anna were taken captive and deported to Nineveh. In Nineveh, Tobit came to the attention of the emperor, who placed Tobit in charge of buying his supplies.

As he was in a position to do so, Tobit always cared for the other Jews in Nineveh. When they were hungry, he shared his food with them. When they needed clothes, he would give them some of his clothes. When they died, he would bury them.

When the emperor died, Tobit and his family fell on hard times. The new emperor did not like the Jews. He murdered many of them, whom Tobit then buried. When the emperor learned that Tobit had buried the bodies, he was furious. Tobit fled, and the emperor confiscated all his possessions. Six weeks later, the emperor was assassinated. Then Tobit returned to Nineveh.

Tobit Goes Blind

One day, tired from burying the dead, Tobit returned home. He lay down in the courtyard and fell asleep. While he was asleep, warm droppings from sparrows in a nest above him fell into his eyes. The droppings caused him to become blind.

Since Tobit was blind, he had to rely on his wife Anna and his son, Tobias, to care for him. Anna worked as a weaver to support the family. One day, she delivered the cloth that she had woven to the customer who had ordered it. The quality of the work so pleased the customer that, in addition to the normal payment, she also received a young goat as a bonus. When Anna returned home with the goat, Tobit, who heard it bleating, thought that she had stolen it. He told Anna to return the goat to its rightful owners. Anna told him that the goat had been a gift.

Tobit's Advice to His Son

One day, Tobit thought that he was about to die. He called his son Tobias to his side to give him some advice. Tobit told Tobias to be sure to bury him when he died. He also instructed him to obey his mother and bury her at his side when she died. He told his son to obey God's laws and avoid sin and the near occasions of sin. He advised his son to be generous in giving to the poor. Tobit let his son know that if he did as he was told, God would bless him. The young man promised to do as his father had commanded him.

Tobias Is Sent to Collect a Debt

After Tobit finished advising his son, he told him that he wished Tobias to travel to the distant city of Rages to collect a debt. His father advised him to find a companion who knew the way to Rages to accompany him on the long journey. Almost as soon as he left the house, Tobias met a young man who was dressed for traveling. Although Tobias did not know it, the "man" was the angel Raphael.

Tobias asked the stranger if he knew the way to Rages. Raphael said that he did know the way, that, in fact, he had been to Rages many times. Tobias took Raphael into his home to meet his father. Raphael told Tobit that he had been to Rages many times and that the roads were safe. He promised to lead the younger man there and back again safely. Tobit blessed them and they departed for Rages.

Tobias Catches a Fish

At the end of the first day, Raphael and Tobias camped on the banks of the Tigris River. As Tobias was washing his feet, a huge fish suddenly jumped out of the river and tried to eat one of his feet! Tobias screamed. Raphael yelled at him not to be afraid and to grab the fish before it got away. Tobias grabbed the monstrous fish and dragged it up onto the riverbank.

Then Raphael ordered Tobias to cut out the fish's liver and gall bladder to be used as medicine. They cooked as much of the fish as they could eat. They salted the rest of the fish and took it with them.

A Fish Suddenly Tried to Eat Tobias' Foot

Tobias Meets Sarah

As they drew near the city of Ecbatana, Raphael told Tobias that they would spend the night in the home of his relative Raguel. Raphael said Raguel had a daughter named Sarah, whom Tobias should marry. Raphael thought that Sarah was smart, brave, and very pretty, and that she would make a wonderful wife.

When Raguel met Tobias and learned who he was, he happily allowed Sarah to marry him. Tobias and Sarah fell in love and were married. Tobias remained with his wife and his father-in-law while Raphael went to Rages to collect the money that was owed.

After Tobias had been with Sarah for a while, he thought about returning to his mother and father. He thought that his father must be worried that he had been gone for so long. At first, Raguel tried to talk Tobias into staying for he had become very fond of his new son-in-law. Yet when he saw that Tobias was determined to leave, he gave Tobias half his property as a wedding present. Then he blessed Tobias and Sarah and sent them on their way.

Tobias Cures His Father

After Tobias, Sarah, and their party had traveled some distance, Raphael told Tobias that he and Tobias should go on ahead of Sarah to prepare the house for her. Thus the two of them left the caravan.

Meanwhile, Tobias' parents had become very worried because they had not heard from their son for quite some time. Every day Anna went to the top of a nearby hill to look for his return. Finally, one day she saw Tobias coming with Raphael.

Anna ran back to her husband and told him that their son had returned. She led Tobit to meet their son. When they met, Tobias took the gall bladder of the fish and applied it to his father's eyes. Immediately Tobit could see again. He threw his arms around his son's neck and wept with joy at the goodness of God's mercy.

The next week, Sarah arrived with the servants and the property that Raguel had given the newly-weds as well as the money that Raphael had collected. The entire family prepared a great feast and there was great rejoicing.

A Gift for an Angel

When the feast was over, Tobias asked his father what reward they should give to Raphael who had done so much for their family. After some discussion, they called Raphael and offered him half of all that they had brought back. Yet, Raphael refused. He told them to pray and give thanks to God for all that He had done for them. Then Raphael revealed his true identity. He told them that he was an angel sent by God to heal Tobit.

When Tobias and his father heard Raphael's words, they were afraid and fell to the ground trembling. However, Raphael assured them that they should not be afraid. It was God's Will that he should come to aid them. He told them to praise God and bless Him as long as they both lived. Then Raphael disappeared. The two men praised God and thanked Him for all the wonderful things that He had done for their family.

With Raphael's Help, Tobias Cures His Father's Blindness

Tobit lived a long and full life. He gave generously to the poor and praised God all his life. He died a holy and peaceful death. Tobias also lived to be an old man. He died at the age of 99 after a long and holy life.

Chapter Review

Fill in the blanks to complete the sentences below.

1. Tobit earned the wrath of the emperor when he _buried all their dead Jews to Nineveh_.

2. The angel _Raphael_ accompanied Tobias to Rages.

3. Tobias used a _gall blater of a fish_ to cure his father's _blindness_.

Chapter 26

A Chronicle of the Kings: The Kings of Judah from Rehoboam to Ahaz

Queen Athaliah Is Ordered to be Taken From the Temple and Executed

A Summary of the Key Events in the Kingdom of Judah from 975 B.C. to the Birth of Our Lord

King Rehoboam reigned from 932 B.C. to 915 B.C. From his death until 587 B.C., eighteen kings (and one queen) ruled the kingdom of Judah. Some of these men were good, holy, and wise rulers. They listened to the prophets whom God sent to them. However, others were quite different. They were evil men and wicked rulers who led their people into sin and idolatry.

To punish the evil kings, in 599 B.C., God allowed the Babylonians to capture Jerusalem. The Babylonians also took the leaders of Judah into captivity. Twelve years later (587 B.C.), the entire population of Judah was taken to Babylon and the kingdom of Judah was destroyed.

The Babylonian Captivity lasted for seventy years (587 B.C. to 517 B.C.). During that time, the Jewish people learned to humble themselves before God and to acknowledge their sins. God did not abandon them, but sent them prophets to strengthen their faith. Finally, with their faith strengthened and their hearts humbled, God caused the Jews to be released from their bondage.

In 538 B.C., God led the Jews out of captivity and back to their own land. They immediately rebuilt the city of Jerusalem and in 517 B.C. completed the Temple, officially ending their period of captivity. For the next two hundred years, they lived in peace.

In 323 B.C., after the death of Alexander the Great, various nations conquered the land of the Jews. There was no peace. Finally, a king named Herod, not one of King David's descendants, ascended to the throne. Now, according to Jacob's prophecy, the time had come for Christ, the Messiah, to be born.

The Kings of Judah from Rehoboam to Ahaz

After King Rehoboam died, his son Abijah became king of Judah. Abijah was a brave ruler and a good general but an evil man. He committed the same sins as his father. After three years, he died and was succeeded by his son, Asa.

Asa was mostly a good and just king. He destroyed many of the pagan temples and worked to abolish idolatry. Like his father, he was a good general and won many victories over his enemies. He ruled for forty-one years. Upon his death, his son Jehoshaphat became king.

Jehoshaphat was a good and holy man. He continued the work of his father Asa. He abolished idolatry and appointed decent, honest men to help him rule the people. For his faithfulness, God gave him victory over his enemies. Jehoshaphat died after a reign of twenty-five years.

Jehoram, Jehoshaphat's son, became king after his father. Unlike his father, Jehoram was a cruel man who worshiped idols. He also failed as a general. After a reign of eight years his son, Ahaziah, succeeded him and ruled for one year before he was killed in battle.

After Ahaziah's death, his mother Queen Athaliah became ruler of Judah. Queen Athaliah was a very wicked woman. Among her most serious sins was to order all the members of the royal family to be murdered. Only Ahaziah's baby son, Joash, managed to escape Athaliah's murderous rampage. Joash's aunt hid him in the Temple for the next six years.

When Joash was seven years old, the high priest of the Temple, Jehoiada, called the royal guards to the Temple. He showed them Joash and told them that Joash was the rightful king. Then Jehoiada anointed Joash king while the royal guard shouted, "Long live the king!"

Queen Athaliah, hearing the noise in the Temple, rushed to the Temple where a crowd had gathered. When she saw King Joash sitting on the throne, surrounded by the people and the royal guard, she screamed, "Treason!" Jehoiada ordered her arrested and taken outside the city and executed.

Jehoiada instructed Joash, who became a good and holy man and a wise ruler. For forty years, Joash ruled Judah. Sadly, some of his officials plotted against him. Two of them murdered him. His son Amaziah succeeded Joash.

Amaziah ruled for twenty-nine years. Once he had established himself in power, he executed the men who had murdered his father. He did not completely destroy the pagan temples, and people continued to worship in them. After twenty-nine years, Amaziah, like his father, was also assassinated. His body was returned to Jerusalem. The people of Judah crowned his sixteen-year-old son, Uzziah, king.

Uzziah was king for fifty-two years but most of them were spent in seclusion. One day Uzziah, wishing to take over the duties of the priests, entered the Temple. He insisted upon burning incense before the Lord, which was the duty of the priests. The priests bravely resisted the threats of the king and ordered him to leave the sanctuary. Uzziah became furious that the priests refused to obey him. He grabbed a censor and threatened to strike one of the priests with it. At that moment, the hand of God struck Uzziah. He was instantly covered with leprosy, a disease he had until he died. His disease forced Uzziah to live apart from the rest of the people. His son Jotham governed the country. When Jotham died, his son Ahaz became king.

Uzziah Was Stricken with Leprosy

Chapter Review

Fill in the blanks to complete the sentences below.

1. The Babylonian Captivity lasted for _seventy years_.

2. For trying to usurp the duties of the priests, God struck King Uzziah with _Leprosy_.

3. _Idolatry_ was the sin most commonly committed by the kings of Judah and Israel.

Chapter 27

The Jews in Babylon: The Kings from Ahaz to the Babylonian Captivity

Angels Attack Assyrian King Sennacherib and His Soldiers

The Evil Ahaz

King Ahaz was one of the most wicked men ever to sit upon King David's throne. Not only did he practice idolatry, he even killed his own son as a burnt offering to the idols! For sixteen years, this vile king ruled over Judah. Then his son Hezekiah ascended to the throne of Judah.

The Holy Hezekiah

King Hezekiah could not have been more unlike his wicked father. Like King David, he did what was pleasing to the Lord. While his father had built up the pagan temples, Hezekiah tore them all down. For his faithfulness, God blessed him and his nation. Hezekiah succeeded in all that he did, and God gave him power over his enemies.

The Assyrian Invasion

In the fourteenth year of Hezekiah's reign, King Sennacherib of Assyria invaded Israel and besieged Jerusalem. Sennacherib demanded a huge tribute, which Hezekiah paid. Nevertheless, the greedy king refused to lift the siege. Hezekiah sent three of his officials to meet with the Assyrians, but they demanded the surrender of the city.

When Hezekiah heard the Assyrian demands, he went to the Temple to pray for God's help. He also sent the Temple priests to Isaiah the prophet to ask him to pray for their deliverance from the hands of the Assyrians. The Lord heard the prayers of Hezekiah and Isaiah.

In the night God sent an angel into the Assyrian camp. The angel killed 185,000 Assyrian soldiers. At dawn the next day, dead bodies littered the camp. The sight of so much death filled Sennacherib with fear. He withdrew his army from Jerusalem and retreated to Nineveh. One day, as he was worshiping his pagan idols, two of his sons murdered him.

Isaiah's Warning

A short time later, King Hezekiah became gravely ill. God sent the prophet Isaiah to see him. Isaiah warned Hezekiah to put his affairs in order because he was going to die. When Hezekiah heard this warning, he became very frightened. He began to pray to God. The Lord heard his prayer and he recovered. For fifteen more years, the people of Judah were blessed by his wise rule. When he died, his son Manasseh became King of Judah.

Isaiah Warns Hezekiah

King Manasseh

Manasseh was only twelve years old when he became king. He reigned for fifty-five years. Sadly, Manasseh was quite unlike his great father. He rebuilt the pagan temples that his father had destroyed. He killed his son as a sacrifice to the pagan idols. Manasseh led the people of Judah to become even more sinful than their pagan neighbors. Manasseh killed so many innocent people that the streets of Jerusalem ran red with blood. For their wickedness, God sent prophets to warn the people that He would punish them for their vile behavior. As a result, God permitted Manasseh to become the captive of the Assyrians who led him away into slavery.

In his captivity, Manasseh saw that he had sinned grievously against the Lord. He turned to the Lord, did penance, and begged for God's help. God took pity on him, answered his prayer, and brought him back to Jerusalem to rule again. In the final years of his life, Manasseh tried to undo the great damage that he had done to Judah and its people.

Amon and Josiah

When Manasseh died, his son Amon became king. He rejected God's law and worshiped idols. He was more sinful than his father had ever been. After two years, officials in his government murdered him. The people of Judah killed the assassins and made Amon's son, Josiah, king.

King Josiah strictly followed God's laws. As king, he worked to abolish idolatry and restore worship of God. Sadly, King Josiah was killed in battle defending his people against the aggression of the Egyptians. His son Joahaz became king. However, Joahaz ruled only a few months before the Egyptians took him as a prisoner to Egypt where he died.

The Babylonian Captivity

Jehoiakim became king next. During his reign King Nebuchadnezzar II of Babylon invaded Judah. For three years, the people lived under the rule of Babylon before they rebelled. When Jehoiakim died, his son, Jehoiachin, became king. Jehoiachin also sinned against the Lord. During Jehoiachin's reign, Nebuchadnezzar II captured Jerusalem. He took Jehoiachin and the entire royal family captive. He deported the royal family, all the leading people, and all the

The Jews Are Taken to Babylon

skilled craftsmen to Babylon. Only the poorest people were left behind in Judah. In addition, Nebuchadnezzar II took away much of the gold and silver that had been given to the Temple over the years.

Nebuchadnezzar II made Zedekiah the king of Judah. Zedekiah was a wicked king who failed to obey God's laws. Yet, he refused to be ruled by the Babylonians. He rebelled against the oppressors. Nebuchadnezzar II returned to Jerusalem with the magnificent Babylonian army. He captured Zedekiah, killed his sons, and took him in chains to Babylon. Then he ordered that Jerusalem and the Temple be destroyed. He also took nearly the entire Jewish population back with him to Babylon.

The Prophet Jeremiah Warns of the Coming Destruction

In the days before the Babylonians destroyed Jerusalem, God sent the prophet Jeremiah to warn the Jews to repent and amend their lives or face the wrath of God. Jeremiah would walk the streets of Jerusalem with a chain around his neck as a sign of the slavery that they would soon have to endure if they did not change their ways. The people cursed him and sought to injure him for his warnings. On one occasion, some royal officials put Jeremiah into a dry well in order to stop him from preaching or even kill him.

When Jerusalem was destroyed and most of the people carried away to bondage, Jeremiah stayed behind to comfort those who remained. He wept amid the ruins of the once great city. Yet

before he died, Jeremiah prophesied that the Lord would restore the people of Israel and Judah to their homeland.

During their time in Babylon, the Jews did penance for their sins. They turned their hearts to God and were sincerely converted to His ways. Nebuchadnezzar treated them well but they longed to return to their own land.

The Prophet Jeremiah

The Jews Mourn in Babylon

Chapter Review

Fill in the blanks to complete the sentences below.

1. During King Hezekiah's reign, the _Assyrians_ invaded Israel.

2. The prophet _Isaiah_ warned King Hezekiah that he was going to die.

3. When King Hezekiah died, his son _Manasseh_ became King of Judah.

4. King _Nebuchadnezzar_ deported the Jewish royal family, all the leading people, and all the skilled craftsmen to Babylon.

5. King _Nebuchadnezzar_ ordered that Jerusalem and the Temple be destroyed.

6. God sent _Jeremiah_ to warn the Jews to repent and amend their lives or they would become slaves.

Chapter 28

God Blesses the Captives: Daniel

The King Orders Shadrach, Meshach, and Abednego into the Fiery Furnace

Daniel and His Three Friends

Among the Jewish captives in Babylon were several young men from the royal family. King Nebuchadnezzar ordered that his prime minister choose some of these young men to serve at the royal court. The young men had to be intelligent, fast learners, and good looking. They were to be taught to read and write the Babylonian language. They would also receive the same food and drink as the members of the Babylonian royal court. Daniel, Shadrach, Meshach, and Abednego were among the young men chosen.

Although receiving the same food as the Babylonian royal family was seen as a great favor to the Jews, Jewish law prohibited Jews from eating several kinds of meat. The four young men, fearing that they would be forced to eat the forbidden meat, went to the guard who had been placed in charge of them. They asked to be fed on vegetables and water for the next ten days. They promised that if they were not stronger and healthier than the men who ate the royal diet, they would agree to eat the forbidden meats. The guard agreed.

After ten days, the four young men were stronger and healthier than those who had been eating the royal food. As a result, the guard allowed them to continue to eat a diet of vegetables and water.

In addition to excellent health, God also blessed the four youths with great wisdom. God also blessed Daniel with the ability to interpret dreams. When the four men were presented to King Nebuchadnezzar, they impressed him more than any of the others to whom he spoke. The men became valuable members of the royal court because they knew more than anyone else in the kingdom. Daniel remained at the Babylonian court until Emperor Cyrus of Persia conquered Babylon.

The Three Young Men in the Fiery Furnace

Some time after the four men entered the king's service, Nebuchadnezzar made a gigantic golden idol. He ordered that everyone in his empire should come to the dedication of the massive statue. He also ordered everyone to worship the huge idol. Anyone who failed to fall down and adore the golden statue would be thrown into a blazing furnace.

At the king's command, everyone fell down and worshiped the idol – except Shadrach, Meshach, and Abednego. (Daniel was not present, but he also would not have worshiped the idol.) Some Babylonians saw that the three young men refused to worship the idol. They spoke to the king and informed him that the three young men were disregarding his orders.

Nebuchadnezzar called Shadrach, Meshach, and Abednego before him. He tried to convince them to worship his statue but they refused. In a rage, he ordered the furnace to be heated seven times hotter than normal. Then he ordered the three men thrown into the fiery furnace. The furnace was so hot that the men who led Shadrach, Meshach, and Abednego to the furnace burst into flame. Shadrach, Meshach, and Abednego walked calmly into the furnace.

As King Nebuchadnezzar looked on, *four* men appeared to be in the furnace. The Lord had sent an angel to protect Shadrach, Meshach, and Abednego! God sent a cool breeze to blow inside the furnace. Not a hair on their heads was singed nor were their clothes burned.

King Nebuchadnezzar approached the furnace and called for the men to come out of the fire. They obeyed. When the king saw that they had not been harmed, he blessed the God of Shadrach, Meshach, and Abednego. King Nebuchadnezzar also decreed that no one should dare say anything offensive about the God of the three young men lest he be killed. Nebuchadnezzar then saw to it that the three young men prospered in Babylon.

Susanna and the Elders

In addition to being revered by the Babylonians, Daniel was greatly respected by the Jewish people for his wisdom. Daniel first came to prominence among the Jews when, on one famous occasion, he saved a young woman from being unjustly put to death. The young woman's name was Susanna.

Susanna and her husband, Joachim, were among the Jewish captives in Babylon. Joachim was a good and honest man. Susanna was considered to be one of the most beautiful women in Babylon.

Two of Joachim's associates were Jewish leaders or *elders*. Unfortunately, they were bad men who used their positions of authority to do evil. One day, their gaze fell upon Susanna, and they determined to do evil with her.

Every day, Susanna would walk in the orchard near her home. The two elders knew where Susanna walked, and one day the two of them accosted her. They said that unless she sinned with them, they would accuse her of various crimes in front of the people.

Susanna did not know what to do. She knew that it would be wrong to sin. Yet she knew if she did not sin, these terrible men would have her killed. She decided that it was better to be killed sinless, than to sin. Thus, she refused to sin with the wicked elders.

The next day, the elders called Susanna before the court. They accused her of some very serious crimes. All her friends and family wept at the disgrace.

The people listened as the elders gave testimony. Since they were leaders of the people, the people believed them. Susanna was condemned to death. In her hour of need, she prayed to God and He answered her prayer.

As the people led Susanna away to be stoned, Daniel, touched by the Holy Spirit, called out that the elders had lied. He demanded that there be another trial.

At the second trial, Daniel had the two elders questioned separately. When Daniel asked the first one where he had

Susanna in Her Magnificent Garden

seen Susanna commit her crimes, he answered, "under a pine tree." When Daniel asked the second elder the same question, he said, "under an oak tree."

When the people heard the two men tell different stories, they realized that the elders were liars. The people knew that the elders had falsely accused Susanna, who was innocent. The people praised God Who had aided those who placed their trust in Him. From that day forward, Daniel had the utmost respect of the Jewish people.

Daniel Proves the Elders are Lying and Saves Susanna

Chapter Review

Fill in the blanks to complete the sentences below.

1. _Shadrach, Meshach, and Abednego_ were thrown into the fiery furnace for refusing to worship an idol.

2. Daniel saved a young woman named _Susanna_ from two evil elders.

3. Daniel saved the young woman by proving that _the the Elders were lying_.

Chapter 29

Into the Lions' Den: Daniel

Belshazzar's Feast

Daniel and King Belshazzar's Feast

After Nebuchadnezzar's death, his grandson, Belshazzar, became ruler of Babylon. One day, he held a great feast to which he invited a thousand of the nobles of the kingdom. As they ate and drank, Belshazzar ordered the golden vessels, which his grandfather had taken from the Temple in Jerusalem, to be brought in so that he and his guests might drink from them. While they were drinking and worshiping their idols, the fingers of a hand suddenly appeared and began to write upon the wall.

Belshazzar became frightened and called for his wise men. He offered a huge treasure to any man who could tell him what the writing on the wall said. Yet, despite the great reward, no one could interpret the handwriting. Then the king sent for Daniel. Daniel had interpreted some dreams for Nebuchadnezzar, so Belshazzar hoped he could interpret the handwriting.

Daniel told the king that the handwriting meant that the days of the Empire of Babylon were numbered and nearly at an end. The Empire of Babylon would be divided between the Medes and Persians. Daniel also said that God had judged Belshazzar and found him deficient.

Later that evening, Daniel's prophecy was fulfilled. The Medes and Persians crept into Babylon during the night. They killed Belshazzar and divided his kingdom. King Cyrus of Persia became the new ruler of Babylon.

In time, Cyrus learned of Daniel and came to appreciate his wisdom. Before long, Daniel became one of Cyrus' most trusted servants and his best friend. Often Cyrus would invite Daniel to have dinner with him.

Daniel and the Idol of Baal

During one of their dinners, Cyrus, who was a decent man, but a pagan, asked Daniel why he did not worship Baal, one of the Babylonian gods. Daniel explained that there was only one God, not a statue made of clay, but the true living God Who created all things. Cyrus replied that Baal *was* a living god. Cyrus knew this to be true because every day Baal ate the food and wine that was left in his temple. At this statement, Daniel laughed. He told Cyrus that he should not be deceived. He pointed out that a statue made of clay and brass cannot eat anything. Cyrus summoned the priests of Baal and repeated Daniel's words to them.

The priests replied that Baal did consume the food and drink provided to him. As proof, the priests of Baal told

Cyrus that he himself should place the food before Baal the next day. Then they would lock and seal the temple door. If in the morning when the door was opened the food were not eaten, then they would willingly be put to death. Cyrus thought this plan a good one, so he ordered it done.

Cyrus told the priests to leave the temple. Then he set the food before the statue of Baal. Daniel, in the presence of the king, put a fine layer of flour on the floor of the temple. Then they closed the door and sealed it.

During the night, as they did every night, the priests of Baal entered the temple by means of a secret door. With their wives and children they gathered up the food and drink that had been placed before the statue and ate it. They failed to notice the flour on the floor.

Early the next morning, Cyrus and Daniel returned to the temple. The seal on the door was intact. When they entered the temple, Cyrus saw that all the food had been eaten. He cried out, "Great is Baal!" However, before Cyrus became too excited, Daniel pointed out the numerous footprints in the flour. Cyrus ordered the temple examined. His men discovered the secret door. When Cyrus saw that he had been deceived, he ordered the priests of Baal to be killed. He allowed Daniel to destroy the statue of Baal and the temple.

Daniel in the Lions' Den

Since the Babylonians were pagans, they worshiped many "gods." Another of their gods was a "dragon"-- probably a very large crocodile. One day, Cyrus told Daniel that the dragon was the true and living god. Cyrus asked Daniel why

Daniel in the Lions' Den

he did not worship the dragon. Daniel replied that the dragon was not a god. In fact, Daniel said he would prove that the dragon was no god. Daniel told Cyrus that he could kill the dragon without a sword or a club. This idea intrigued Cyrus, so he gave Daniel permission to try. Daniel boiled tar and fat together and added hair. Then he made balls of the mixture and fed them to the dragon. When the dragon ate the volatile mixture, it burst into flame and was burnt to ashes.

When the Babylonians heard what Daniel had done to their "god," they were furious. They demanded that Cyrus turn Daniel over to them. At first, Cyrus refused. However, the mob became so violent that Cyrus finally had no choice but to give Daniel to the angry mob. The Babylonians threw Daniel into a pit filled with hungry lions in the hope that they would eat Daniel. Yet the Lord kept the lions' mouths closed. Daniel remained unhurt.

After six days in the pit with the lions, Daniel became hungry. At this time, living in the ruins of Jerusalem, there was a prophet named Habakkuk. Habakkuk had just made a pot of soup that he was taking to some men working in the fields outside the city. As he walked to the fields, an angel appeared to Habakkuk. The angel told him to take his pot of soup to Daniel who was in the lions' den.

Habakkuk had no idea what the angel was talking about. He had never been to Babylon and had no idea where the lions' den was. So the angel grabbed Habakkuk by his hair and whisked him off to Babylon and placed him in the lions' den with Daniel.

Daniel ate the dinner that God had miraculously provided. He thanked God for His protection, His kindness, and for remembering him in his distress. Then the angel returned Habakkuk to Jerusalem.

After Daniel had been in the lions' den for seven days, King Cyrus came to see what had become of him. He found Daniel sitting quietly in the middle of the pack of lions. When Cyrus saw this miracle he was amazed. He immediately ordered Daniel to be pulled from the lions' den and his persecutors to be thrown in. Daniel's tormenters had barely been put into the den before the ravenous lions attacked them. King Cyrus later published an edict in which he commanded all his subjects to venerate Daniel's God, because He was the one true living God.

The Jews Return from Captivity

The miracle in the lions' den caused Cyrus to appreciate Daniel's wisdom and advice even more. Daniel became one of the emperor's closest advisors. It was through Daniel's efforts that Cyrus finally agreed to free the Jews from captivity and allow them to return home.

After the Jews had been in captivity for the seventy years foretold by the prophets, God, using Daniel as His instrument, touched the heart of Emperor Cyrus of Persia. In 538 B.C., Cyrus ordered the Jews to return to Jerusalem and rebuild the Temple. Under the leadership of Sheshbazzar, more than forty-two thousand Jews returned from exile. Cyrus was very generous to the exiles. He gave them money and returned the sacred gold and silver vessels that King Nebuchadnezzar had taken from the Temple.

After seven months, the Jewish people had settled back in their towns. They assembled in Jerusalem and built an altar where they could offer sacrifices until the Temple could be rebuilt. For the next twenty-one years, the Jews worked to rebuild the Temple. When it was finally completed, the people wept with joy and offered sacrifices to the Lord.

Twenty years after the first group of exiles returned to Jerusalem, a prophet named Ezra escorted another group of Jews back from Babylon to their native land. Ezra and the prophet Nehemiah worked among the people teaching them about God's law. The two prophets also labored to stop the pagan practices that the people had begun while living with the Babylonians. Nehemiah also urged the people to rebuild the city of Jerusalem. The people embraced this plan so enthusiastically, that they rebuilt the walls of the city in less than two months. Before long, the entire city had been rebuilt.

Nehemiah Rebuilds Jerusalem

Chapter Review

Fill in the blanks to complete the sentences below.

1. Daniel interpreted the handwriting on the wall for *Belshazzar*.

2. The Babylonians worshiped a *dragon* that Daniel killed.

3. When Daniel was in the lions' den, God sent *Habakkak* with a pot of soup.

4. Why did Cyrus believe that Baal was a living God? *Cyrus believed that Baal was a living God because the preist's of Baal ate the food that was infront of him.*

5. How did Daniel prove Cyrus was wrong? *By puting flour on the ground and seing footprints on the ground.*

6. Through Daniel's efforts, *Cyrus* finally freed the Jews from captivity and allowed them to return home.

Chapter 30

A Shield for Her People: Esther

Esther Becomes Queen

When Cyrus freed them, not all of the Jews returned to Judah. The great kindness that the kings of Persia had shown to the Jewish people caused many of them to remain in Babylon. One of those who stayed was a woman named Esther.

The ruler of Persia at this time was King Xerxes. During a certain banquet he was giving for his nobles, he ordered his wife Queen Vashti to come to the banquet. Vashti was a very beautiful woman and King Xerxes wanted to show her off to his guests. However, the queen was having her own banquet and refused to come. Her refusal made Xerxes furious. He ordered that Queen Vashti be exiled. He also told his advisors to find him another wife who would be a better queen.

In Babylon, there lived a Jew named Mordecai who had a niece named Esther. Esther was a lovely young woman whom Mordecai had adopted and raised after her parents had died. Esther was one of the women the king's advisors chose to be presented to him. The royal advisors took her to the palace where they prepared her to meet King Xerxes. Following Mordecai's advice, Esther kept her Jewish faith a secret.

To make sure no harm befell Esther, Mordecai kept watch outside of the palace every day. When the royal advisors presented Esther to King Xerxes, he fell in love with her. They married and he made her his queen. Then he gave a great banquet in Esther's honor.

King Xerxes' Feast

Mordecai Saves the King

Even after Esther became queen, Mordecai continued to watch over her to ensure her safety. One day while Mordecai was keeping watch, he discovered a conspiracy. Two of the king's servants planned to murder Xerxes. Instantly, Mordecai warned Esther of the plot. She immediately told her husband who launched an investigation. When Xerxes discovered the truth of the report, he had the two men executed. Xerxes ordered this event recorded in the official history of the empire.

Haman's Plot

Some time later, King Xerxes appointed a man named Haman to be his Prime Minister. All the officials were ordered to show their respect to Haman by bowing before him. Everyone did so, except Mordecai. When Haman noticed this, he became extremely angry. He determined to punish Mordecai. When he learned that Mordecai was a Jew, Haman decided to kill all the Jews in the Persian Empire.

In order to accomplish his evil scheme, Haman told King Xerxes a terrible lie. Haman said that the Jews planned to revolt against Xerxes. This lie convinced King Xerxes to publish an edict declaring that all Jewish men, women, and children were to be killed on the same day.

When Mordecai heard this edict, he rushed to Esther and urged her to go to King Xerxes and beg for the lives of her people. However, there was an impediment. There was a law, which forbade anyone to enter the king's presence unless the king called for him or her. Anyone entering the king's presence unbidden would be put to death. The only exception occurred if the king held out his golden scepter to the person. In that case, the person's life would be spared. King Xerxes had not sent for Esther in a month.

Esther's Banquet

Esther prayed and fasted for three days. At the end of the three days, she put on her most beautiful dress. Then she went, unbidden, to see Xerxes. When

Xerxes Extends His Scepter

King Xerxes saw her, he extended his golden scepter to her. He asked her what she wanted. She replied that she wanted to invite him and Haman to be her guests at a banquet she was preparing for the following evening. Xerxes promised that he and Haman would attend.

That night, Xerxes could not sleep. In order to quiet his mind, he ordered the official history of his reign to be read to him. Eventually the reader came to the section about the conspiracy to murder Xerxes that Mordecai had discovered. Xerxes asked if Mordecai had ever been rewarded for his service. When Xerxes was told that he had not been rewarded, Xerxes called for Haman. He asked Haman what should be done for a man that the king wished to reward.

Haman thought that Xerxes meant him. So he replied that a man the king wished to honor should first be clothed in royal robes. Then he should be placed on the king's finest horse while the most noble of the king's ministers walked before him shouting, "See how the king rewards someone he wishes to honor!" King Xerxes ordered Haman to provide these honors for Mordecai. Haman got the robes and the horse and he himself led Mordecai through the streets shouting, "See how the king rewards someone he wishes to honor!"

Esther Accuses Haman

Soon it was time for Queen Esther's banquet, and Haman hurried to attend. During the feast, Xerxes asked Esther what she wanted. He promised to give her anything even if she asked for half his kingdom. Esther revealed that she was a Jew. She asked only for her life and the lives of her people. She assured Xerxes that the Jews did not intend to revolt. When Xerxes heard how he had been tricked and his confidence abused he became furious. He asked who had been responsible for daring to do such a thing. "Haman," Esther answered.

Xerxes jumped up in a fury. He called in his advisors and asked what he should do. One of them told the king that Haman had just built a gallows at his house that was seventy-five feet high from which he planned to hang Mordecai. "Hang Haman on it," Xerxes ordered.

The Jews Defend Themselves

That very night, Haman was hanged from his own gallows. Xerxes gave Mordecai all of Haman's lands and his titles. Esther begged the king to revoke his order allowing the Jews to be killed. Xerxes said that once a decree was made, it could not be revoked; however, he said that he would issue another decree saying that the Jews could organize and defend themselves.

When the day came for the Jews to be attacked according to the first decree, the Jews were ready. They defended themselves against their attackers. They killed many of their enemies including Haman's ten sons.

For the rest of his life, Mordecai served as Xerxes' Prime Minister. Mordecai was honored and liked by his fellow Jews. He worked for their welfare and the welfare of their descendents.

Chapter Review

Fill in the blanks to complete the sentences below.

1. King Xerxes married Esther after _Queen Vashti_ refused to come to his banquet.

2. _Mordecai_ was Esther's uncle.

3. _Haman_ wanted to kill Esther's uncle.

4. What did Xerxes do when he learned he had been tricked? _He had Haman hanged_ _He became furious and asked who had been responsible for daring to do such a thing._

5. How did King Xerxes reward the man who had saved his life? _By clothing him in royal robes, then he placed on the king's best horse while the most noble of the king's ministers walked before him shouting "See how the king's rewards someone he wishes to honor!"_

A Sword for Her People: Judith

Judith

Holofernes Brings a Holocaust

Soon after the Jews had returned to Judah and rebuilt the Temple, Holofernes, an Assyrian general, invaded their lands and threatened them. Holofernes marched into

Judah at the head of a vast and powerful army. He had so many soldiers that his army covered the land like a swarm of locusts. Holofernes captured many of the cities of Judah. He killed many of the people he captured. He burned the crops and slaughtered the livestock. Everyone was terrified of him.

Eventually Holofernes and his massive army reached the town of Bethulia. There, he besieged the town. He cut off the town's water supply. After thirty-four days, the town ran out of water. The people began to despair and talked of surrendering to Holofernes. They felt it would be better to live as slaves than to die of thirst. Then the town leader spoke to them. He urged them to wait five more days. If God did not send them aid in five days, then he would agree to surrender the town.

The Strength of Judith

Within Bethulia, there lived a beautiful young widow named Judith. When she heard what the town elder had said, she went to see him. She told him that he could not surrender the town because if Bethulia fell to Holofernes then Jerusalem and the Temple would also fall. The elder agreed with her but said that he could not go back on his promise. He asked her to pray for rain.

Judith told the elder that she would do something that the Jewish people would never forget. She told the elder to leave the town gate unlocked and to let her and her maid leave the town that night. He agreed.

Judith returned home and prayed to God for strength. Then she dressed herself in her finest clothes. She put on her best jewels and her best perfume. Thus attired, she and her maid walked to the Assyrian camp.

Judith in the Assyrian Camp

Already a very attractive woman, God added to Judith's beauty. When Holofernes saw her, her loveliness astonished him. He told her not to be afraid. He ordered a tent to be set up for her. He gave her access to all of the camp and allowed her to leave the camp each morning to pray. For three days, Judith lived in the Assyrian camp.

On the fourth day after Judith's arrival in Holofernes' camp, he gave a magnificent banquet for his highest-ranking officers. He ordered his servant to invite Judith to the banquet. She accepted. Judith's presence at the banquet caused Holofernes to drink more alcohol than he ever had before. Late at night, the guests left and Holofernes, who was very drunk, threw himself on his bed and fell asleep. Judith was left alone in the tent with the unconscious general.

Judith Slays Her Enemy

Judith stood near Holofernes' bed and prayed to God for the strength to destroy her enemy. Then she drew Holofernes' sword from its scabbard that hung on his bedpost. Grabbing his long hair, she chopped off his head.

Judith put Holofernes' head in a bag and gave it to her maid. Then the two women left the Assyrian camp as they always did when they went to pray. They crossed the valley and returned to Bethulia. She assembled the town leaders and the

Judith with the Head of Holofernes

people and showed them Holofernes' head. Everyone was totally amazed. Judith told them to praise the Lord Who had protected her and delivered their enemy into her hands. Everyone bowed down and worshiped God.

The next morning, the people hung the head on the town walls. They gathered up their weapons and rushed out to attack the Assyrians. When his officers went to wake Holofernes, they found only his headless body. Soon the entire Assyrian camp panicked. As a result, the Assyrians were easily overcome. All of Israel rejoiced in the victory.

Judith spent the remainder of her life in Bethulia. From this time forward, she was famous throughout Israel. Many men wanted to marry her, but she never remarried. When she died, she was buried next to her husband. All of Israel mourned her passing.

Chapter Review

Fill in the blanks to complete the sentences below.

1. Holofernes commanded the _Assyrians_ army.

2. Eventually, Holofernes and his army reached the town of _Bethulia_, where Judith lived.

3. Judith told the town leader that he could not surrender the town to Holofernes because if their town fell then _Jerusalem and the Temple would fall._.

4. Judith killed Holofernes with his _sword_.

To Live Free or Die: The Maccabees

The Maccabees Gather Their Followers about Them.

The Terror of Antiochus

From 336 to 323 B.C., Alexander the Great conquered almost all of the known world. Alexander was the greatest military commander of his time and perhaps of all time. None of the empires he faced could stand against him. The greatest empire was that of Persia. When Alexander defeated Emperor Darius of Persia, it become part of his empire. When Alexander died, his generals divided his empire.

In 169 B.C., one of the descendents of one of Alexander's generals, Antiochus IV, marched with a massive army against Israel and the city of Jerusalem. After a few years, Antiochus had captured most of Israel. Antiochus began a reign of terror in Israel. He banned the practice of the Jewish faith. He burned the sacred texts and forbade the people to obey the Law. He set up pagan temples and altars. He defiled the altar in the Jewish Temple. In the face of death, many began to worship at the pagan shrines and sacrifice to the pagan gods. However, others died rather than worship idols.

Among those martyred for their faith were a woman and her seven sons. When Antiochus ordered them to eat pork, a meat forbidden by Jewish law, they refused. They told the king that they would rather die than break the Laws of God. Their refusal infuriated Antiochus. He ordered the seven brothers to be beaten. Yet the men still refused to obey.

Then the evil Antiochus tortured and killed the oldest son. He asked the next oldest son if he would eat pork. He refused. The king tortured and killed him and then his brothers until only the youngest brother remained. On the youngest brother, the king tried a new approach. He promised the young boy honor and riches if only he would eat the forbidden food. Yet the king's treasures and promises could not seduce him. Finally, Antiochus urged his mother to persuade her son to save his life and renounce his religion. However, she encouraged him to be worthy of his six dead brothers.

Enraged, Antiochus ordered the youngest son to be tortured more cruelly than his older brothers. Finally, he too died. Lastly, the evil king murdered the mother.

The Maccabees Launch a Guerilla Campaign

Many suffered martyrdom under Antiochus, but there was one family who chose to fight the tyrant rather than submit to his cruelty. In Judah, there lived a priest named Mattathias who had five sons. The cruelty of Antiochus appalled him. Eventually, Antiochus' soldiers came to the city of Modein, where Mattathias and his sons lived, to organize pagan sacrifices. Not only did Mattathias refuse to sacrifice, but when he saw a fellow Jew coming forward in front of the entire town to sacrifice, Mattathias was filled with a righteous anger. Mattathias leapt forward and killed the man on the pagan altar. Then he killed the soldier who was forcing them to sacrifice and tore down the altar.

Mattathias was now determined to free his country from its oppressor. Going through Modein, he called upon any Jew who wished to be free and defend God's Law to follow him. He fled with his sons and his supporters into the mountains. There he began to wage a campaign of guerilla warfare against Antiochus.

At first, Mattathias and his men merely destroyed the pagan altars and temples. However, as more and more devout and patriotic men joined his group, he began to do more. About a year later, when Mattathias died, leadership of the small army of Jews fell to his son Judas.

Judas was brave and an excellent military leader, which made him the logical choice to succeed his father as commander of the Jewish forces. In the early days of the revolt, Judas had been given the nickname "Maccabee." The nickname meant "the hammer" and referred to his bravery and ferocity in battle. His followers were called the Maccabees.

The Maccabees Capture Jerusalem

Under the leadership of Judas Maccabee, the Maccabees defeated all the forces that Antiochus sent against them.

Judas Maccabee Defeats His Enemies

When they had defeated their enemies, Judas told his brothers that they should retake Jerusalem and purify the Temple. They tore down the old altar which Antiochus had desecrated then built and consecrated a new altar. For eight days the people celebrated the dedication of the Temple and the victories of Judas Maccabee.

Antiochus' Just Punishment

When Antiochus heard of the Maccabees' success, he was furious. He gathered his army and decided to lead it to Jerusalem, which he planned to turn into a graveyard full of Jews. Yet as soon as he had made these plans, God struck him down. Antiochus was seized with terrible stomach pains. However, he refused to leave his chariot. He ordered his driver to drive even faster. As a result, he fell out of the chariot and hurt himself very badly.

The wounds from Antiochus' fall began to fester. Worms began to crawl in them. His entire body began to petrify. The smell was so bad that the entire army became sick and no one could go near him. He suffered unspeakable agony. It was a fitting punishment for a man who had tortured so many.

In his anguish, Antiochus began to realize that he had sinned grievously against the Lord. As he felt his death approach, he tried to make a bargain with God to save his life. He promised that he would not destroy Jerusalem and murder all the Jews there. He promised to undo the evils he had done and even become a Jew himself. Tragically, his prayer was not sincere and he could not escape God's just punishment. King Antiochus IV died a frightful death, all alone, in the mountains of a foreign land. He left the world a fearsome example of God's righteous justice.

Independence for Judah

After the death of Antiochus IV, his son, Antiochus V, assembled an army of over 120,000 men and 32 war-elephants to reconquer Judah. Putting their faith in God, Judas and his army sallied forth to meet them. During the middle of the night, Judas launched a sneak attack upon the enemy camp and killed almost two thousand men.

Later, the two forces clashed again. In the middle of the battle, Judas' brother, Eleazar, saw that one of the war-elephants wore royal armor. He thought that King Antiochus must be riding this elephant. Eleazar boldly ran through the enemy troops toward the elephant. His sword flashed in the sun as he cut down any soldier who stepped in his path. The mighty war-elephant was heavily armored all over its body. Only one spot remained unprotected. Eleazar ran underneath the elephant and drove his spear deep into the massive animal's unprotected belly. The elephant died, crushing Eleazar.

The Death of Eleazar

After many victories, Judas Maccabee won the independence of his country. Sadly, many Jews died in the fighting. However, when the bodies of these dead Jews were examined, it was discovered that under their coats they carried small pagan idols. Then everyone knew why these men had been killed. When Judas saw why they had been punished, he called upon his men to pray for their fallen comrades that their sinful act might be forgiven. He also took up a collection from his men of twelve thousand silver drachmas, which he sent to Jerusalem for prayers to be offered for the sins of the dead. "It is therefore a holy and wholesome thought to pray for the dead, that they may be loosed from sins." 2 Macc. 12:46

The Death of Judas Maccabee

In 160 B.C., an enormous Assyrian army again invaded Judah. Judas and his army marched to meet them. When his men saw the size of the army that faced them, they were very afraid and began to desert. In fact, so many men deserted that only 800 soldiers remained with Judas.

Despite being vastly outnumbered, the lion-hearted Judas urged his men to attack. His men begged him to retreat and return later with reinforcements. Yet Judas would not run from a battle. He told them that if their time had come to die, they should die bravely.

Judas led his small band into battle against the Assyrians. At first, the Jews were victorious. They crushed their enemies. However, the weight of numbers finally began to tell. In the middle of the fiercest fighting, Judas was struck down. His remaining few soldiers fled.

The Scepter Passes from the Kingdom of Judah

After the death of Judas, his brother Jonathan became ruler of Judah. Jonathan was also an excellent military leader. He defeated the Assyrians and won a number of other victories. Jonathan made peace treaties with Rome and Sparta.

After the death of Jonathan, his brothers each led the nation. Under their rule, peace was established and Judah began to flourish. Alas, their successors were not the measure of these men and did not follow God's Law as the Maccabees had. The Jews, as they had so often in the past, drifted away from God and into sin.

After the Maccabees, the nation fell into civil war. There was unrest everywhere. Violence replaced peace. As a last resort, the Jews asked the Romans to come in and attempt to settle the differences between the two sides. Soon, however, the Romans had filled Judah with their armies. They seized control of the government. In 47 B.C., Roman Emperor Julius Caesar appointed Antipater head of the government. Antipater made his oldest son governor of Jerusalem and his next son, Herod, governor of Galilee.

Herod gained the Romans' goodwill by successfully putting down some violent uprisings. An invasion of Judah caused him to flee to Rome where he met the future Caesar Augustus who, along with the Roman Senate, named him King of Judah. Of course, the Jews refused to accept a king appointed by the Romans. It was not until 37 B.C., that Herod, with Roman help, conquered his kingdom (Judah) and returned to power.

Thus ended the kingdom of Judah. The scepter had passed from the tribe of Judah. According to the prophets, this was the time when the Messiah, the Savior, would come to save mankind and bless the world.

Chapter Review

Fill in the blanks to complete the sentences below.

1. In 169 B.C., King _Antiochus_ marched with a massive army against Israel and the city of Jerusalem.

2. Among those martyred for their faith by this evil king were a woman and her _seven sons_ who refused to _eat pork_ .

3. To fight this evil king, _Mattathias_ and his five sons began a guerilla campaign.

4. The eldest of the five sons was Judas who had been given the nickname _Maccabee_ , which meant "hammer."

5. How did the king in Question #1 die? _fell from chariot first With terrible stomach pains and worms began to crawl in him_

6. Judas' brother Eleazar died when _he killed a war-elephant and it crushed him_ .

7. The Jews asked _Romans_ to help them end the civil war and settle their differences.

8. _Herod_ became king of Judah with Roman assistance.

117

Answer Key

Chapter 1
1. eternal
2. the Tree of Life/the Tree of Knowledge of Good and Evil
3. rib or side
4. Lucifer
5. Michael

Chapter 2
1. serpent
2. a Redeemer
3. Cain
4. Mount Ararat
5. rainbow

Chapter 3
1. nephew
2. bread/wine
3. special pledge
4. a pillar of salt
5. the Dead Sea

Chapter 4
1. Isaac
2. Eliezer
3. Rebecca

Chapter 5
1. Jacob/Esau
2. Esau/Jacob
3. Jacob
4. Jacob
5. Jacob/Israel

Chapter 6
1. twelve
2. a coat of many colors
3. Potiphar
4. baker/cupbearer
5. corn/cows

Chapter 7
1. Benjamin
2. spies
3. money

Chapter 8
1. silver cup
2. Judah
3. Goshen
4. Israelites

Chapter 9
1. Saudi Arabia
2. the house where they were eating fell on them
3. Job
4. God restored all that Job had lost two times over.

Chapter 10
1. in the Nile River
2. "saved from the waters"
3. killed a man
4. burning bush
5. Aaron
6. blood

Chapter 11
1. 10
2. the Angel of Death (or death of every first born)
3. cloud/fire
4. the Red Sea
5. quails/manna
6. Joshua

Chapter 12
1. Mount Sinai
2. Honor thy father and thy mother
3. Seventh Commandment
4. golden calf
5. Holy of Holies/Sanctuary
6. Ark of the Covenant
7. the Holy Eucharist

Chapter 13
1. Passover
2. Pentecost
3. Levites/the Tabernacle
4. 40

5. because he doubted God (and struck the rock twice)

Chapter 14
1. Joshua
2. Jericho
3. Jacob (or Israel)
4. Gideon, Samson, and Samuel.
5. Deborah

Chapter 15
1. Baal
2. Midianites
3. trumpet/jar with a torch inside

Chapter 16
1. Philistines
2. lion
3. three hundred foxes
4. one thousand Philistines
5. Delilah
6. pulled down the central pillars of the Temple of Dagon

Chapter 17: Judge and High Priest: Samuel
1. Hannah/Eli
2. in battle (God punished the Israelites for disobedience)
3. in the Temple of Dagon
4. God sent disasters
5. Boaz

Chapter 18
1. Saul
2. Samuel
3. harp
4. Goliath

Chapter 19
1. spear
2. Jonathan
3. a piece of cloth/a spear
4. suicide (fell on his own sword)

Chapter 20
1. Jerusalem
2. the Ark of the Covenant
3. Uriah
4. Absalom

5. he was a man of war and blood
6. Solomon

Chapter 21
1. wisdom
2. Sheba
3. to please his wives
4. He would divide the Kingdom of Israel

Chapter 22
1. Israel/Judah
2. Ahab/Jezebel
3. Baal/bull/fire

Chapter 23
1. Naboth
2. a fiery chariot
3. Naaman/leprosy
4. bringing a man to life after he died

Chapter 24
1. Nineveh
2. the belly of a whale

Chapter 25
1. buried the dead Jews
2. Raphael
3. fish/blindness

Chapter 26
1. seventy years
2. leprosy
3. Idolatry

Chapter 27
1. Assyrians
2. Isaiah
3. Manasseh
4. Nebuchadnezzar II
5. Nebuchadnezzar II
6. (the prophet) Jeremiah

Chapter 28
1. Shadrach, Meshach, and Abednego
2. Susanna
3. the elders had lied

Chapter 29
1. King Belshazzar
2. dragon

3. Habakkuk
4. He thought that Baal ate the food set before it
5. He put flour on the temple floor and caught the priests
6. Cyrus

Chapter 30

1. Queen Vashti
2. Mordecai
3. Haman
4. He had Haman hanged
5. Mordecai was clothed in royal robes; placed on the king's finest horse, while Haman walked before him shouting "See how the king rewards someone he wishes to honor!"

Chapter 31

1. Assyrian
2. Bethulia
3. Jerusalem and the Temple would also fall
4. sword

Chapter 32

1. Antiochus
2. seven sons/eat pork
3. Mattathias
4. Maccabee
5. fell from his chariot and died from wounds he sustained
6. he stabbed a war elephant in its belly and it fell on him
7. the Romans
8. Herod